MW01612432

The Print Handwriting Workbook For Teens

belongs to:

Aron Hernandez

This Print Handwriting Workbook is divided into the following parts:

Part 1:
Trace and practice letters a-z and A-Z

Part 2:
Writing three letter words

Part 3:
Writing four letter words

Part 4:
Writing five letter words

Part 5:
Writing words starting with a Capital letter

Part 6:
writing Numbers and Numbers Words 1- 20

Part 7:
Writing sentences and motivational quotes

Part 1:
Learning Letters

Trace the letters and practice writing them in the remaining space

Are you ready ?
Let's go

A	B	C	D	E	F	G	H	I	J	K	L	M	N	O	P	Q	R	S	T	U	V	W	X	Y	Z

Starting at number 1,
trace the letter by
following the order
of numbered circles

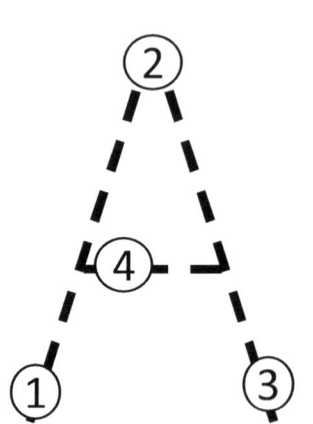

Trace the letters using the example above.

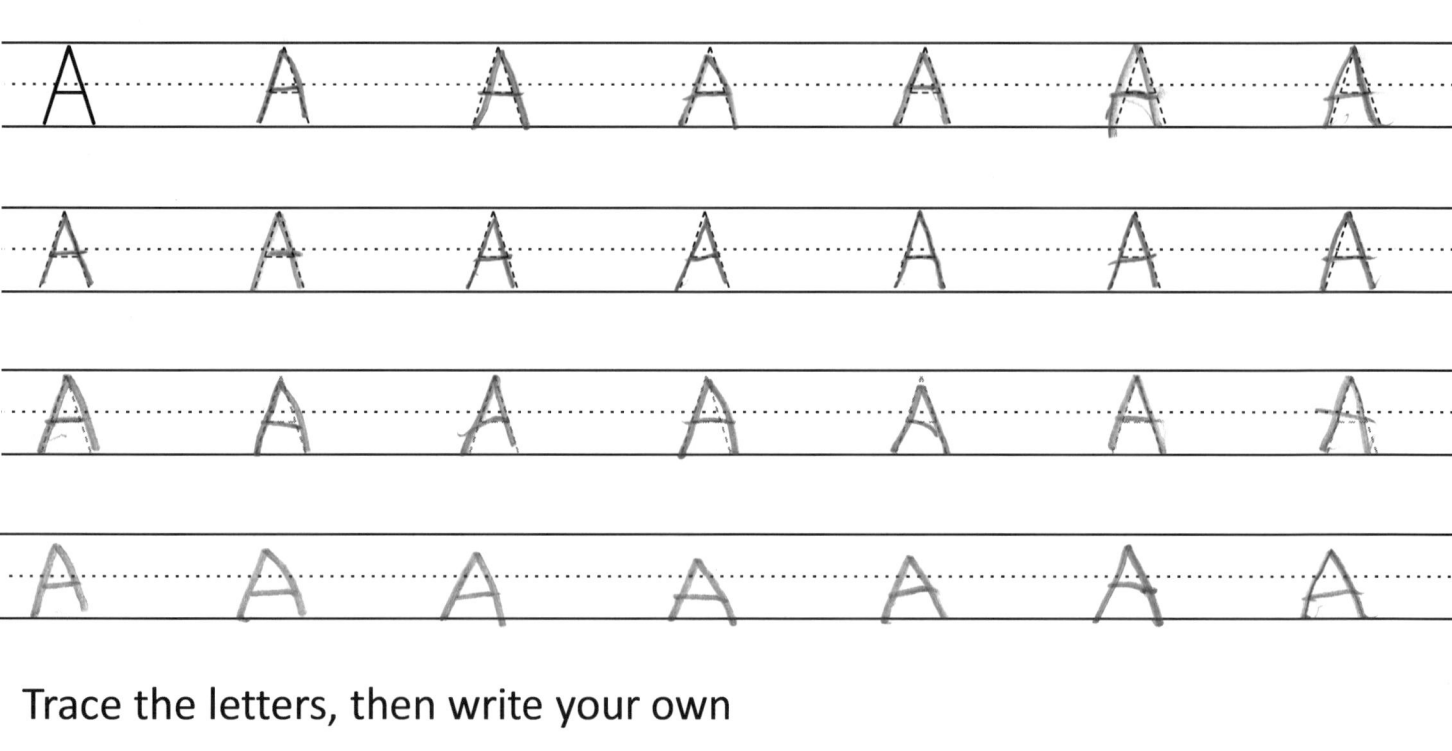

Trace the letters, then write your own

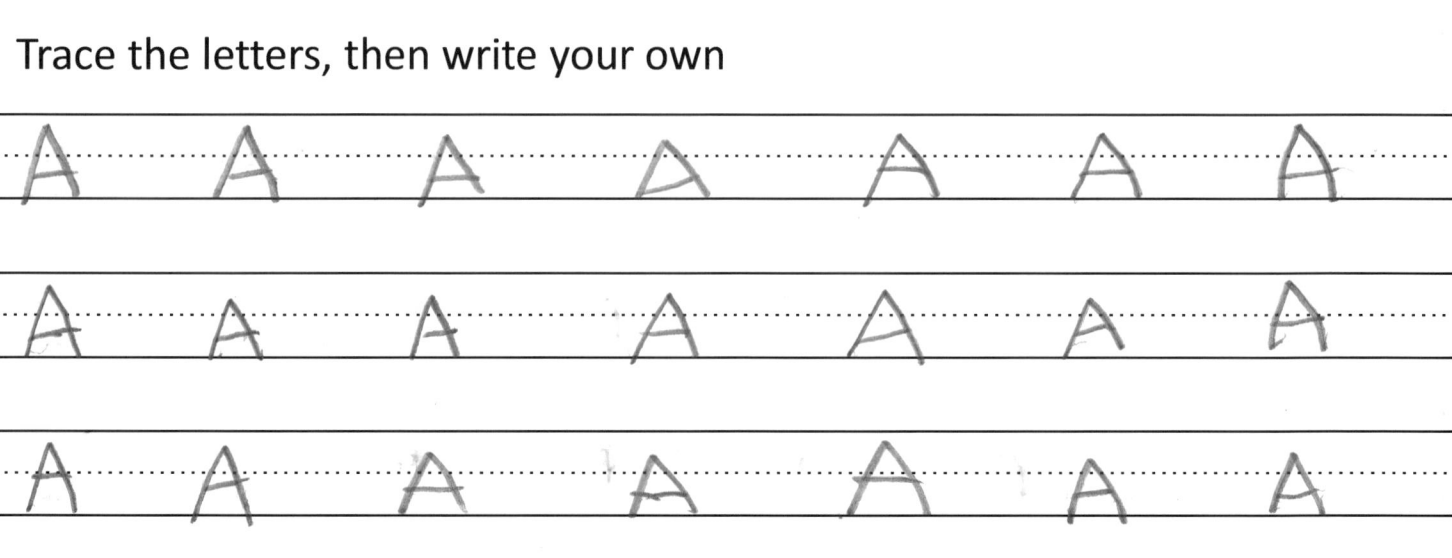

a	b	c	d	e	f	g	h	i	j	k	l	m	n	o	p	q	r	s	t	u	v	w	x	y	z

Starting at number 1, trace the letter by following the order of numbered circles

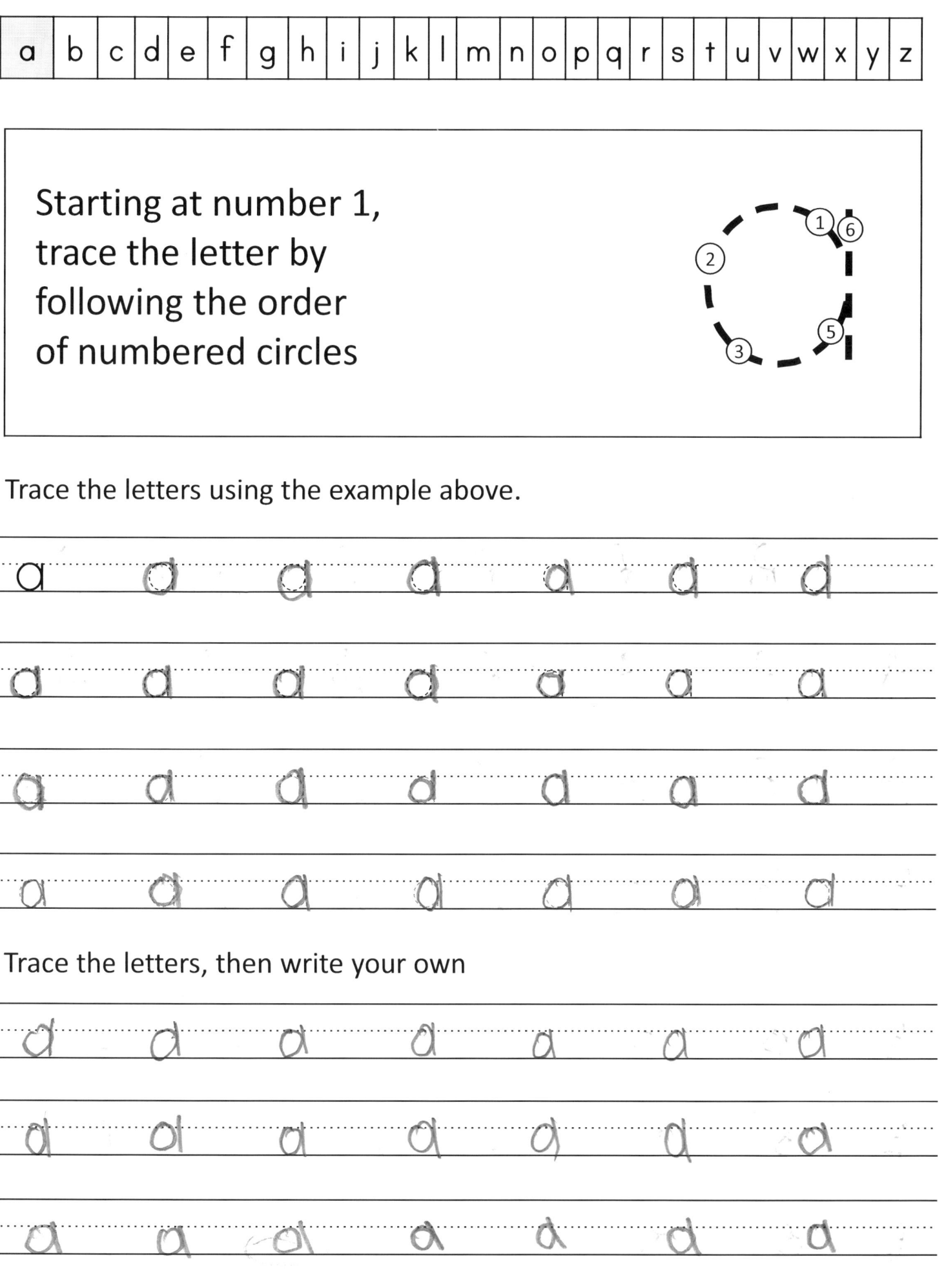

Trace the letters using the example above.

Trace the letters, then write your own

A	B	C	D	E	F	G	H	I	J	K	L	M	N	O	P	Q	R	S	T	U	V	W	X	Y	Z

Starting at number 1, trace the letter by following the order of numbered circles

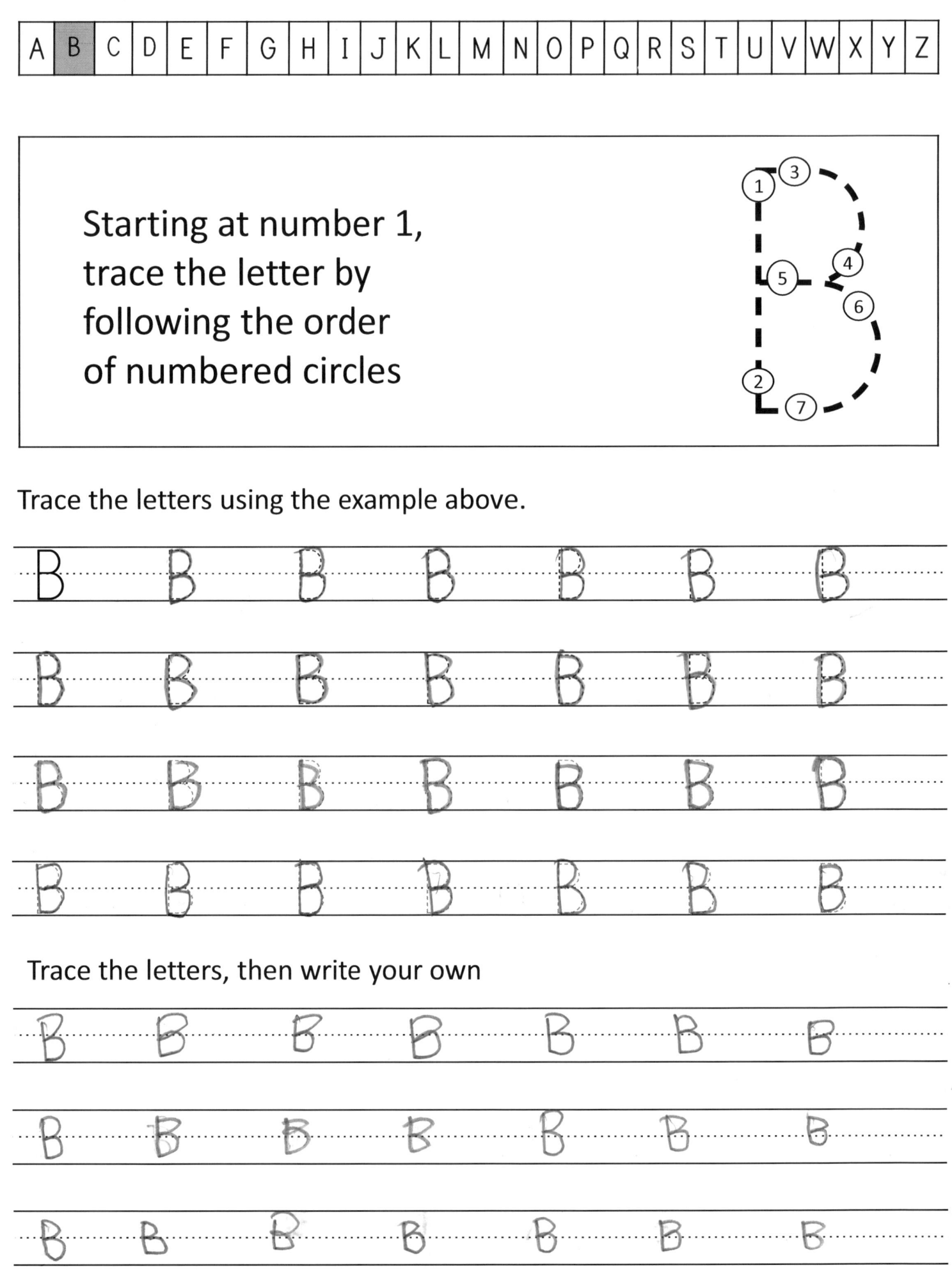

Trace the letters using the example above.

Trace the letters, then write your own

| a | b | c | d | e | f | g | h | i | j | k | l | m | n | o | p | q | r | s | t | u | v | w | x | y | z |

Starting at number 1,
trace the letter by
following the order
of numbered circles

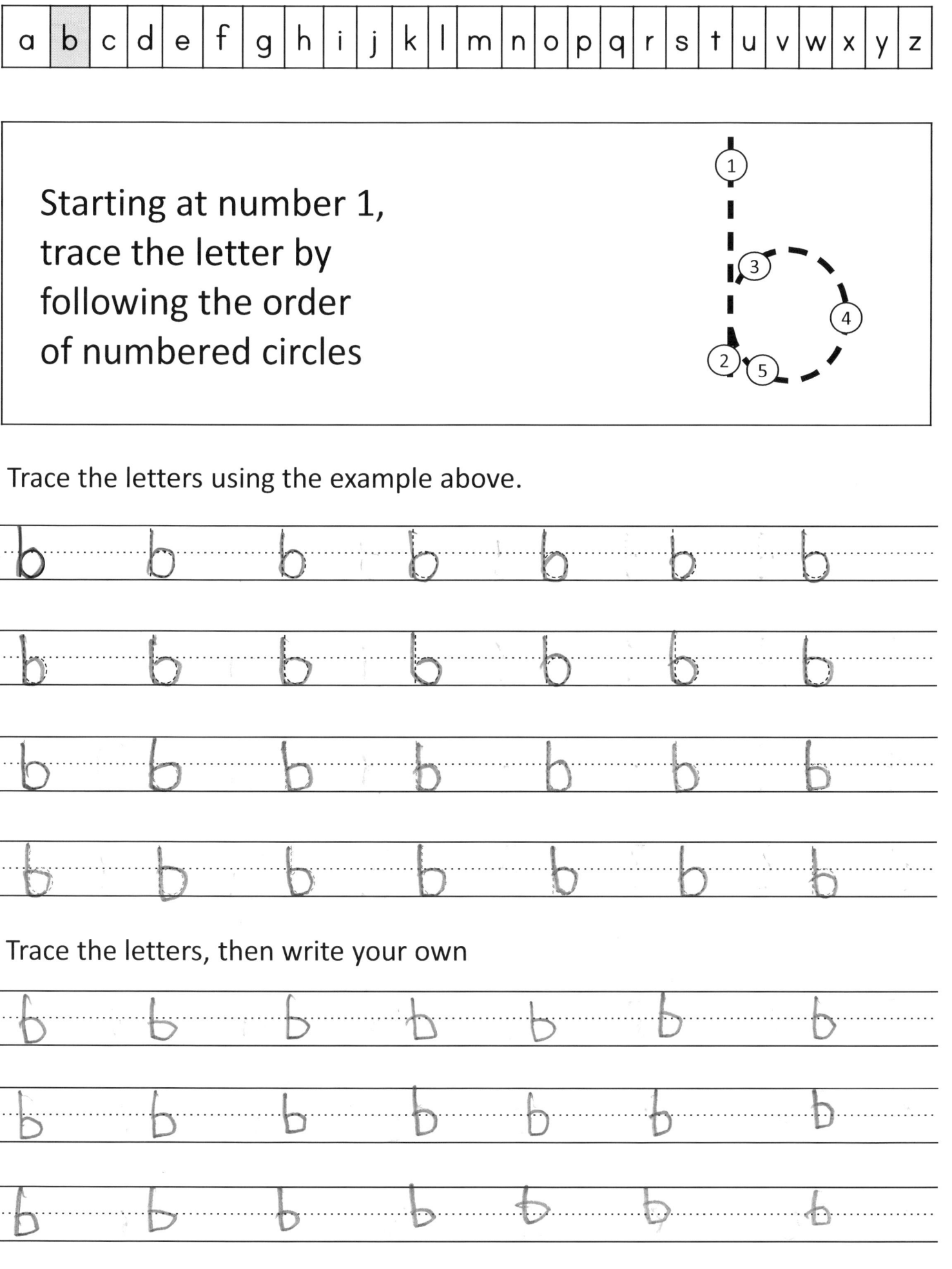

Trace the letters using the example above.

Trace the letters, then write your own

| A | B | C | D | E | F | G | H | I | J | K | L | M | N | O | P | Q | R | S | T | U | V | W | X | Y | Z |

Starting at number 1,
trace the letter by
following the order
of numbered circles

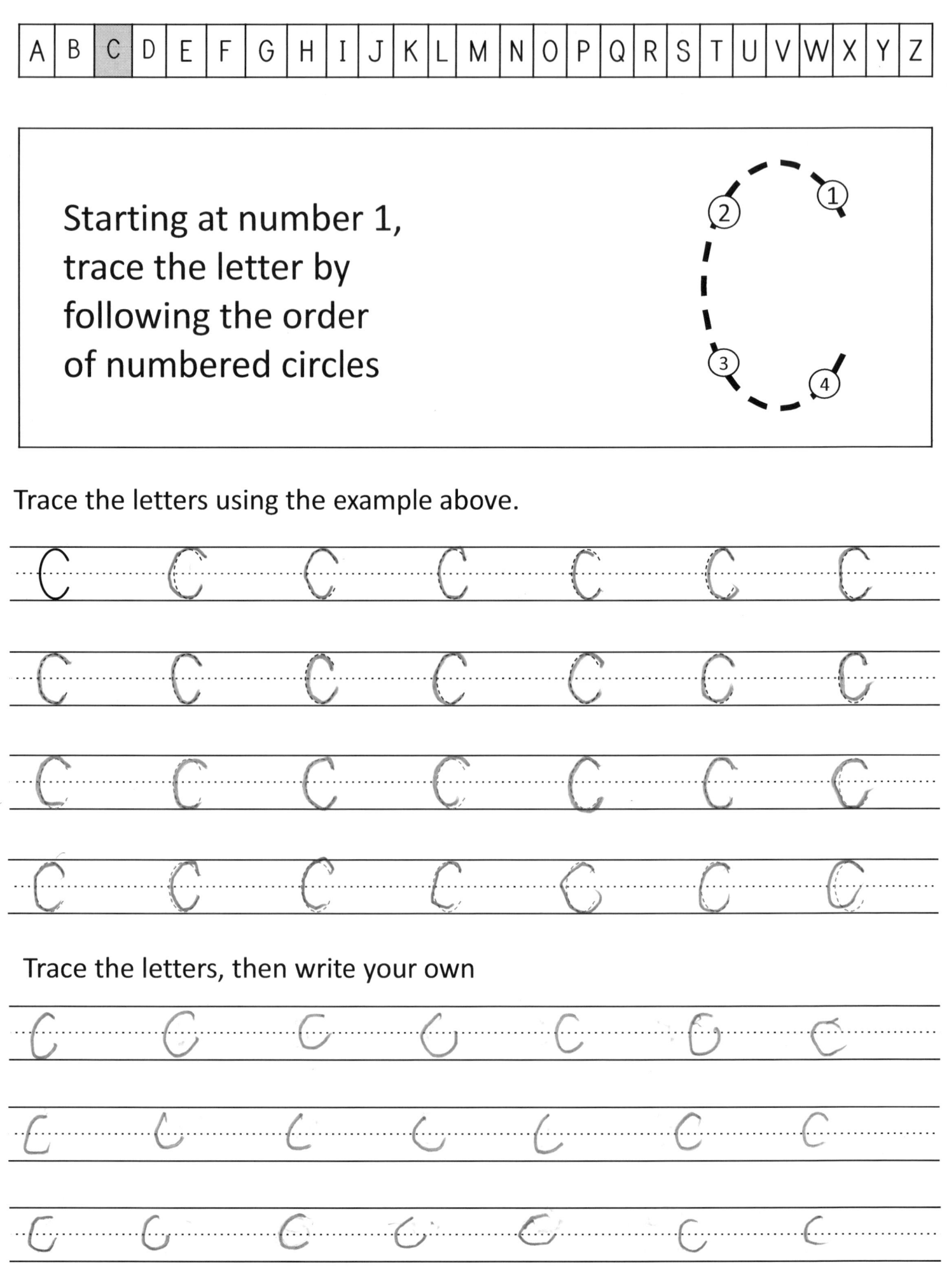

Trace the letters using the example above.

C C C C C C C

C C C C C C C

C C C C C C C

C C C C C C C

Trace the letters, then write your own

C C C C C C C

C C C C C C C

C C C C C C C

a	b	c	d	e	f	g	h	i	j	k	l	m	n	o	p	q	r	s	t	u	v	w	x	y	z

Starting at number 1, trace the letter by following the order of numbered circles

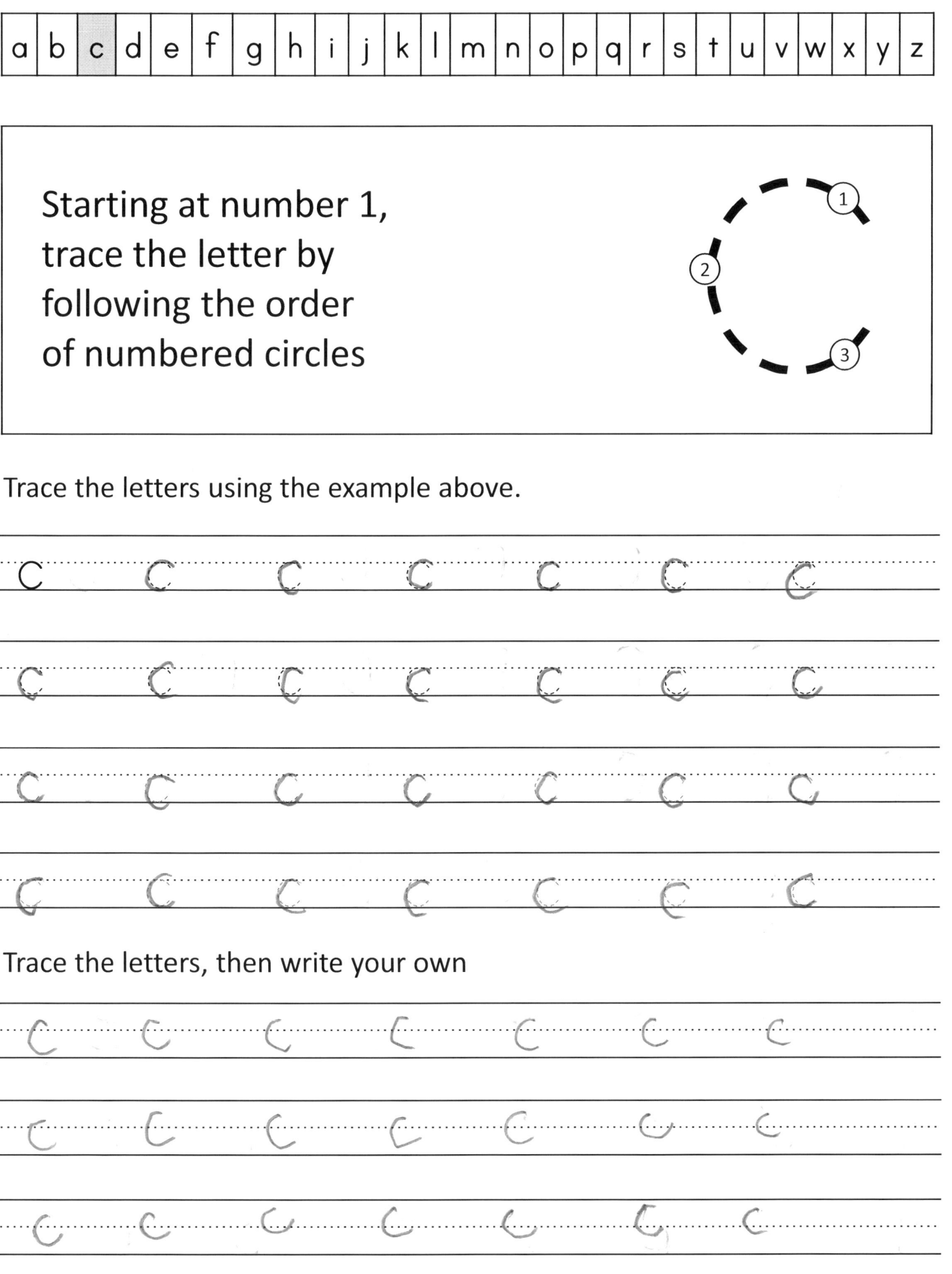

Trace the letters using the example above.

Trace the letters, then write your own

A	B	C	D	E	F	G	H	I	J	K	L	M	N	O	P	Q	R	S	T	U	V	W	X	Y	Z

Starting at number 1, trace the letter by following the order of numbered circles

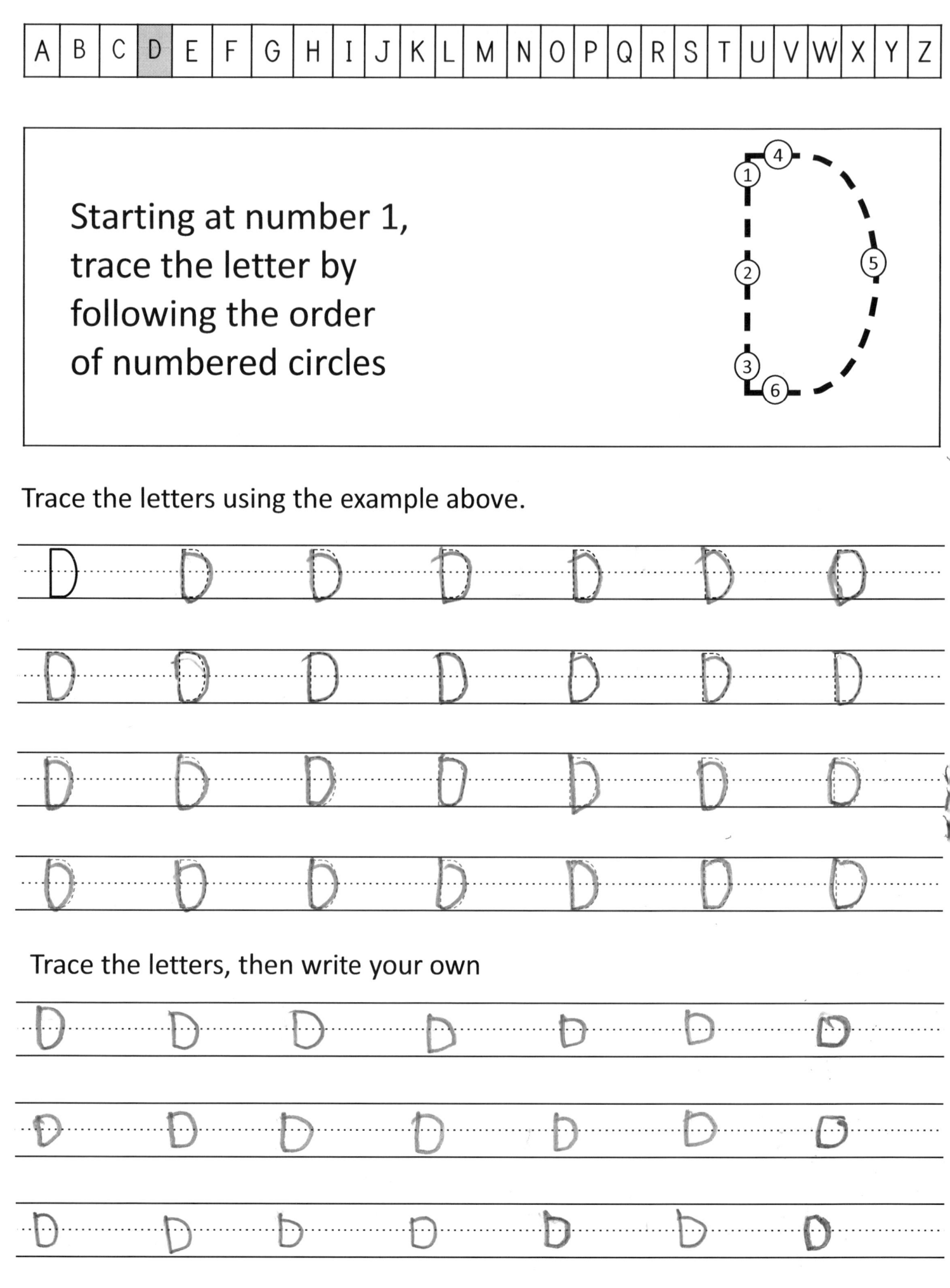

Trace the letters using the example above.

D D D D D D D

D D D D D D D

D D D D D D D

D D D D D D D

Trace the letters, then write your own

D D D D D D D

D D D D D D D

D D D D D D D

a	b	c	d	e	f	g	h	i	j	k	l	m	n	o	p	q	r	s	t	u	v	w	x	y	z

Starting at number 1, trace the letter by following the order of numbered circles

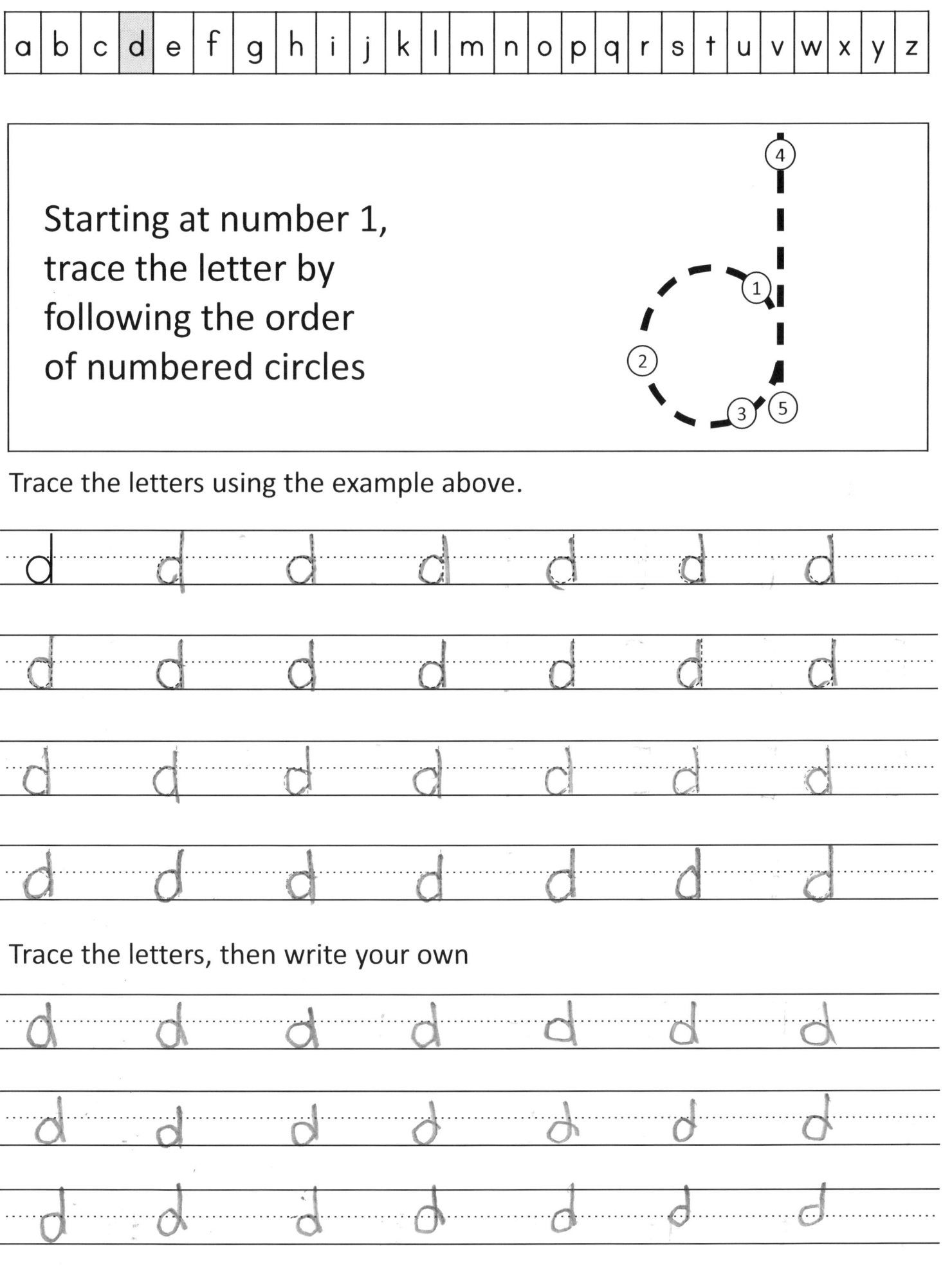

Trace the letters using the example above.

Trace the letters, then write your own

| A | B | C | D | E | F | G | H | I | J | K | L | M | N | O | P | Q | R | S | T | U | V | W | X | Y | Z |

Starting at number 1, trace the letter by following the order of numbered circles

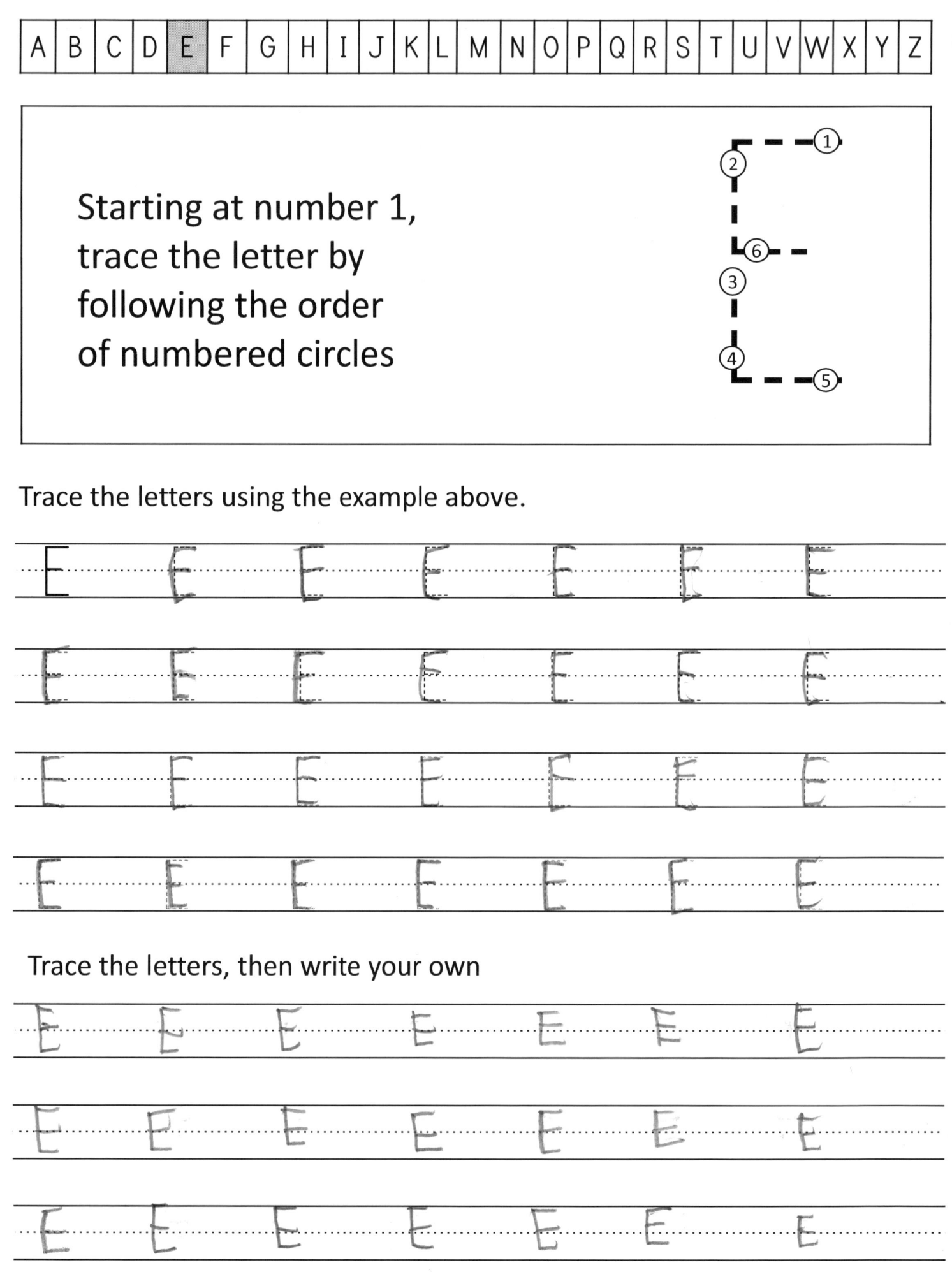

Trace the letters using the example above.

E   E   E   E   E   E   E

E   E   E   E   E   E   E

E   E   E   E   E   E   E

E   E   E   E   E   E   E

Trace the letters, then write your own

E   E   E   E   E   E   E

E   E   E   E   E   E   E

E   E   E   E   E   E   E

a	b	c	d	e	f	g	h	i	j	k	l	m	n	o	p	q	r	s	t	u	v	w	x	y	z

Starting at number 1,
trace the letter by
following the order
of numbered circles

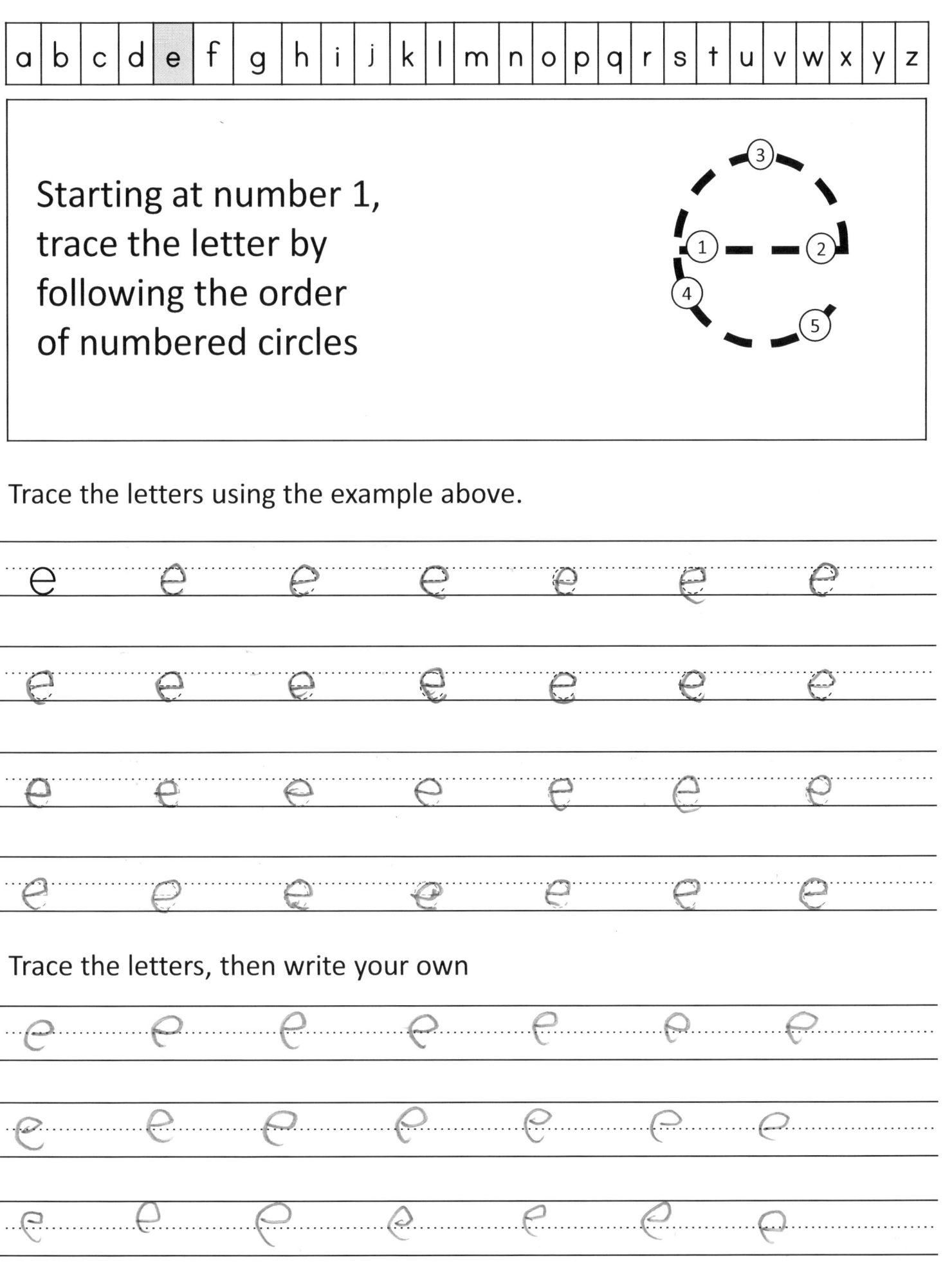

Trace the letters using the example above.

Trace the letters, then write your own

Starting at number 1, trace the letter by following the order of numbered circles

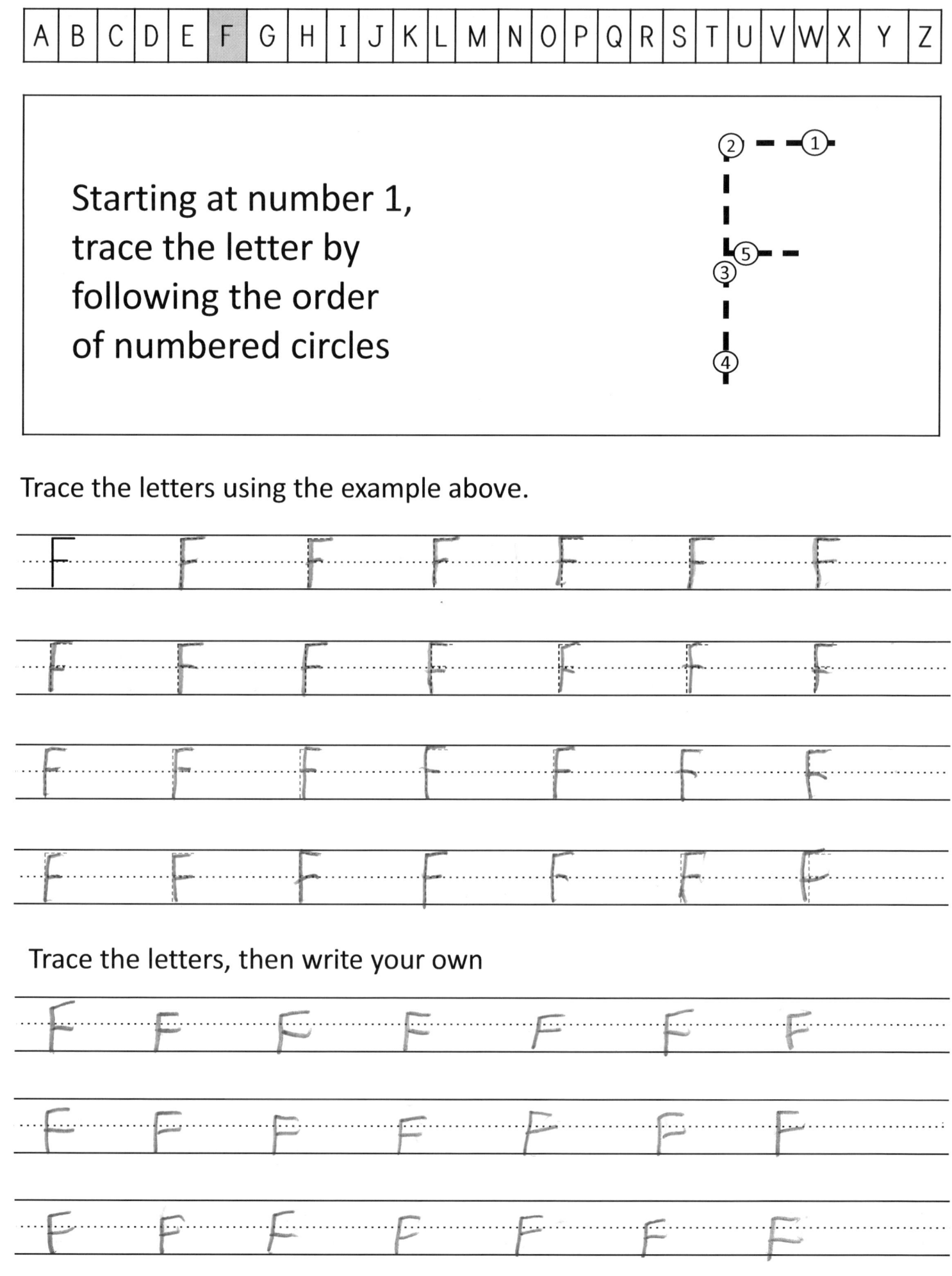

Trace the letters using the example above.

F F F F F F F F

F F F F F F F F

F F F F F F F F

F F F F F F F F

Trace the letters, then write your own

F F F F F F F

F F F F F F F

F F F F F F F

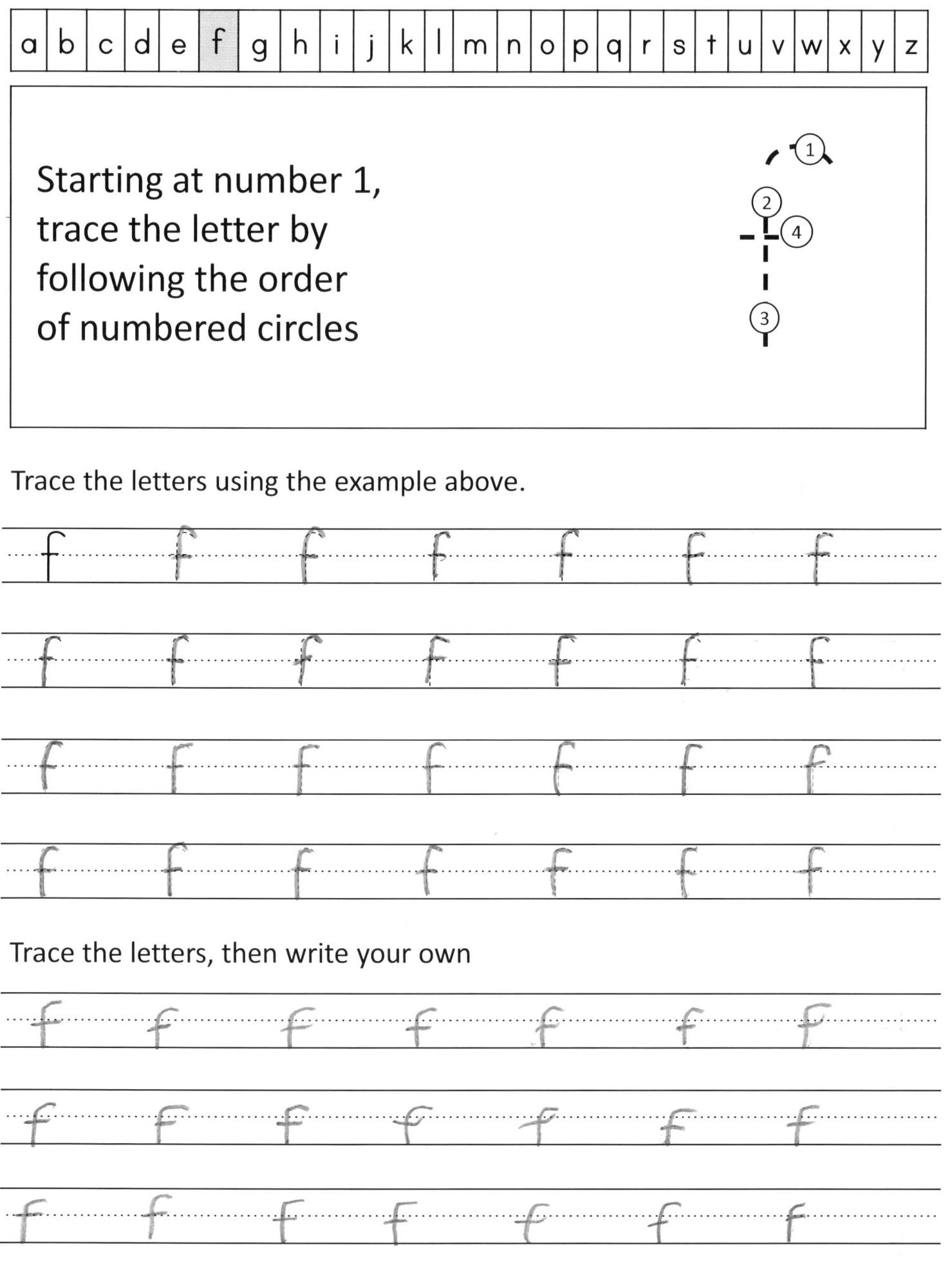

| a | b | c | d | e | f | g | h | i | j | k | l | m | n | o | p | q | r | s | t | u | v | w | x | y | z |

Starting at number 1,
trace the letter by
following the order
of numbered circles

Trace the letters using the example above.

f   f   f   f   f   f   f   f

f   f   f   f   f   f   f   f

f   f   f   f   f   f   f   f

f   f   f   f   f   f   f   f

Trace the letters, then write your own

f   f   f   f   f   f   f

f   f   f   f   f   f   f

f   f   f   f   f   f   f

| A | B | C | D | E | F | G | H | I | J | K | L | M | N | O | P | Q | R | S | T | U | V | W | X | Y | Z |

Starting at number 1, trace the letter by following the order of numbered circles

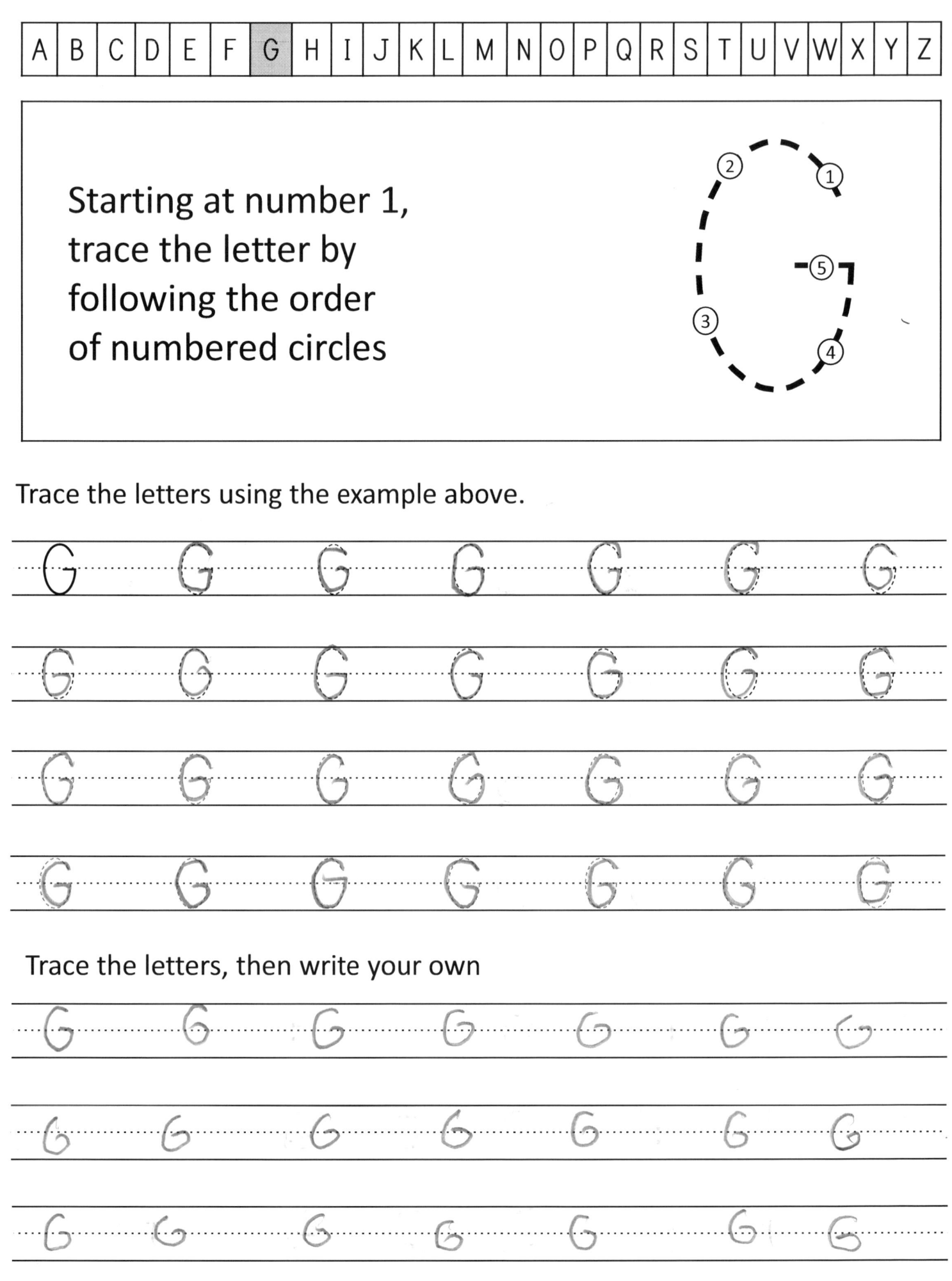

Trace the letters using the example above.

G G G G G G G

G G G G G G G

G G G G G G G

G G G G G G G

Trace the letters, then write your own

G G G G G G G

G G G G G G G

G G G G G G G

| a | b | c | d | e | f | g | h | i | j | k | l | m | n | o | p | q | r | s | t | u | v | w | x | y | z |

Starting at number 1,
trace the letter by
following the order
of numbered circles

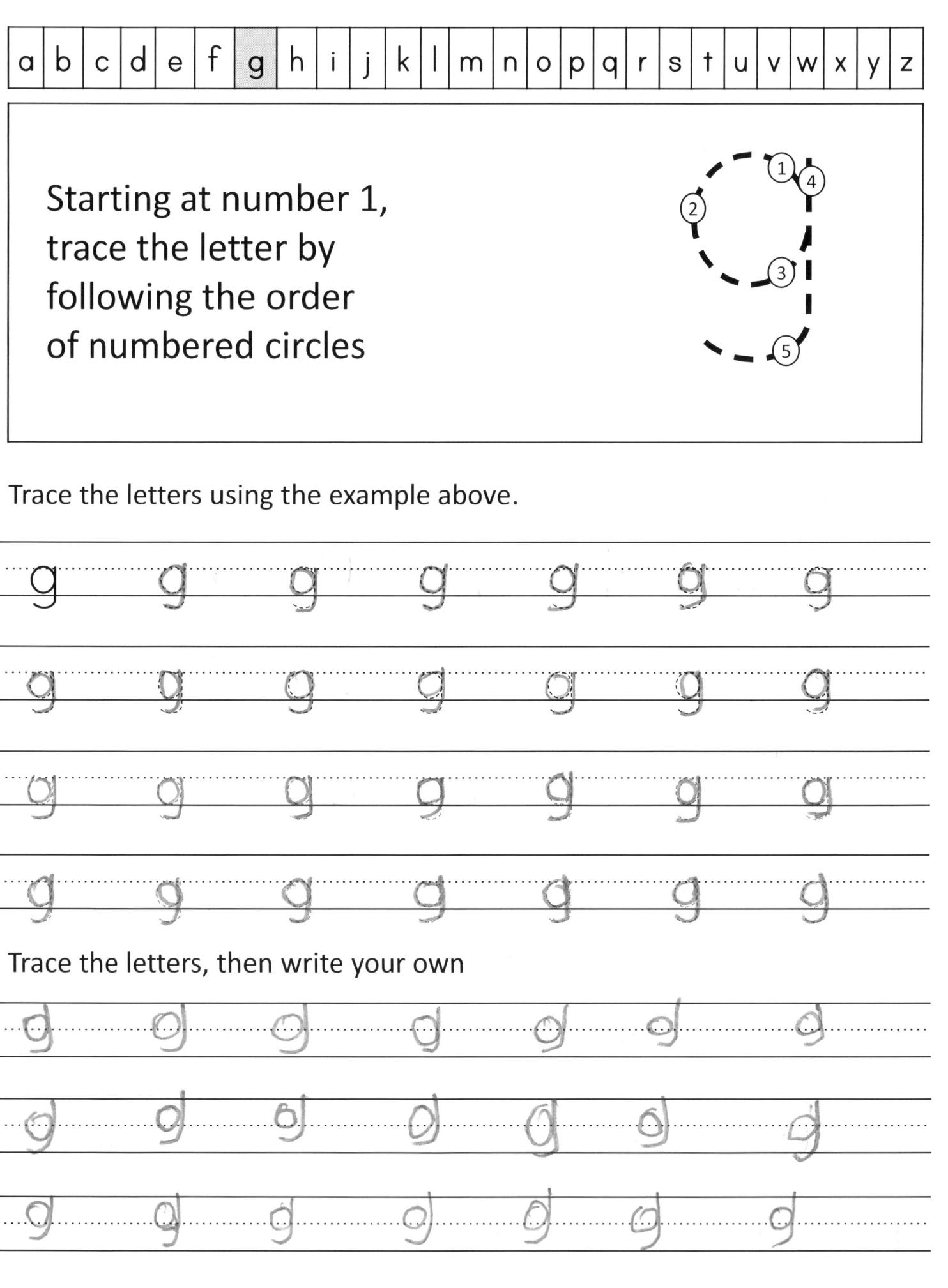

Trace the letters using the example above.

Trace the letters, then write your own

A	B	C	D	E	F	G	H	I	J	K	L	M	N	O	P	Q	R	S	T	U	V	W	X	Y	Z

Starting at number 1, trace the letter by following the order of numbered circles

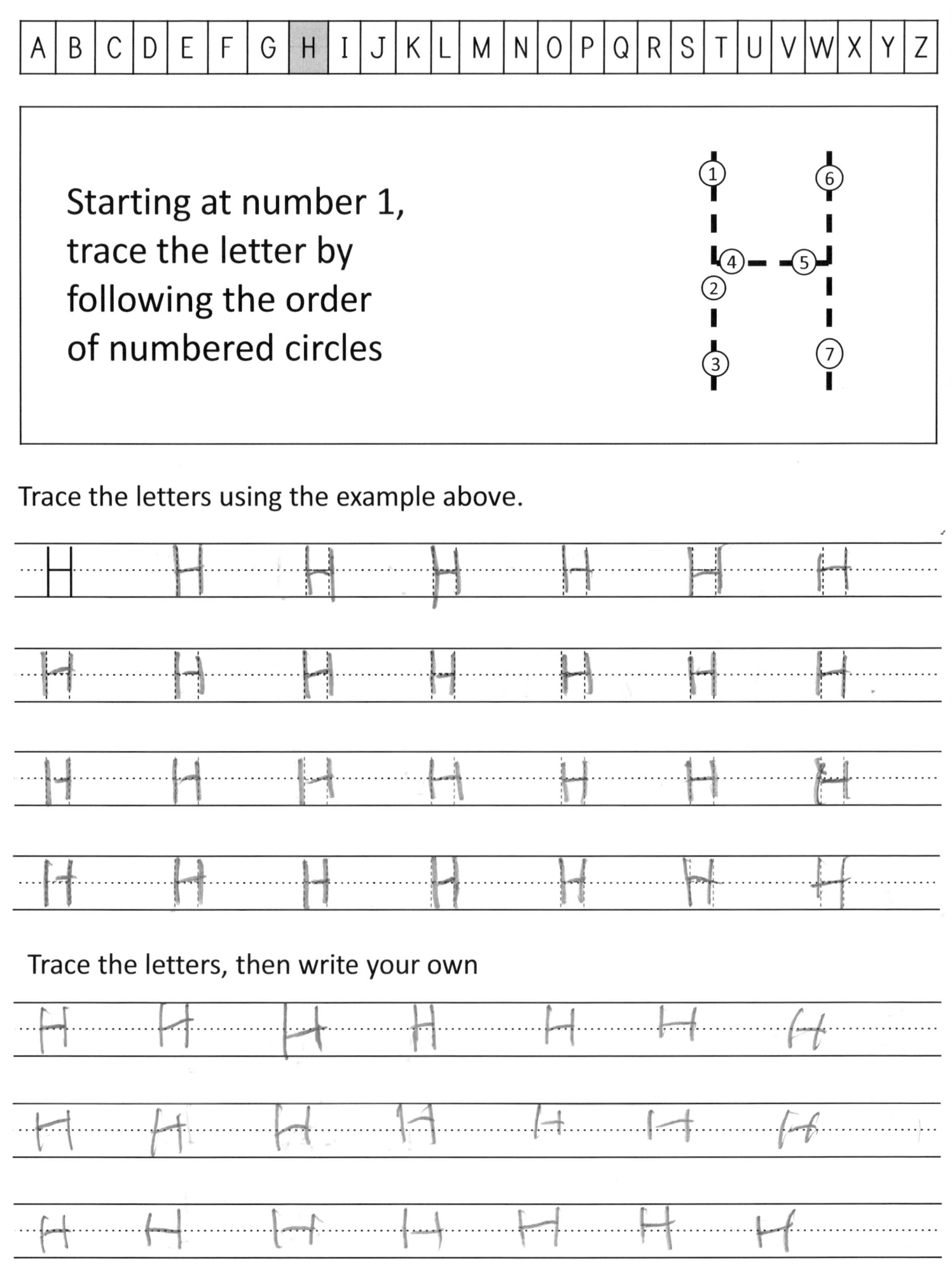

Trace the letters using the example above.

Trace the letters, then write your own

| a | b | c | d | e | f | g | h | i | j | k | l | m | n | o | p | q | r | s | t | u | v | w | x | y | z |

Starting at number 1, trace the letter by following the order of numbered circles

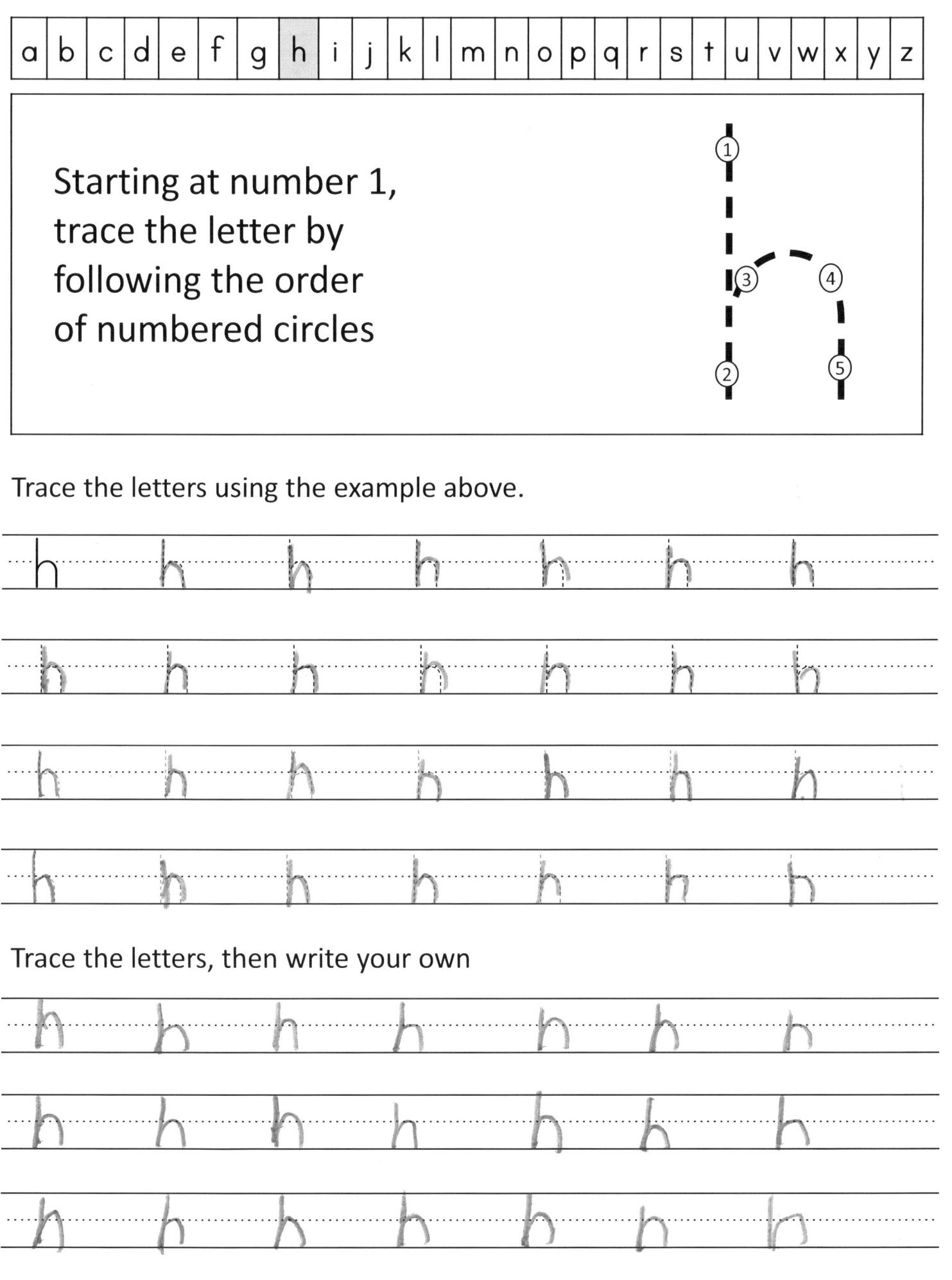

Trace the letters using the example above.

Trace the letters, then write your own

A	B	C	D	E	F	G	H	I	J	K	L	M	N	O	P	Q	R	S	T	U	V	W	X	Y	Z

Starting at number 1,
trace the letter by
following the order
of numbered circles

Trace the letters using the example above.

Trace the letters, then write your own

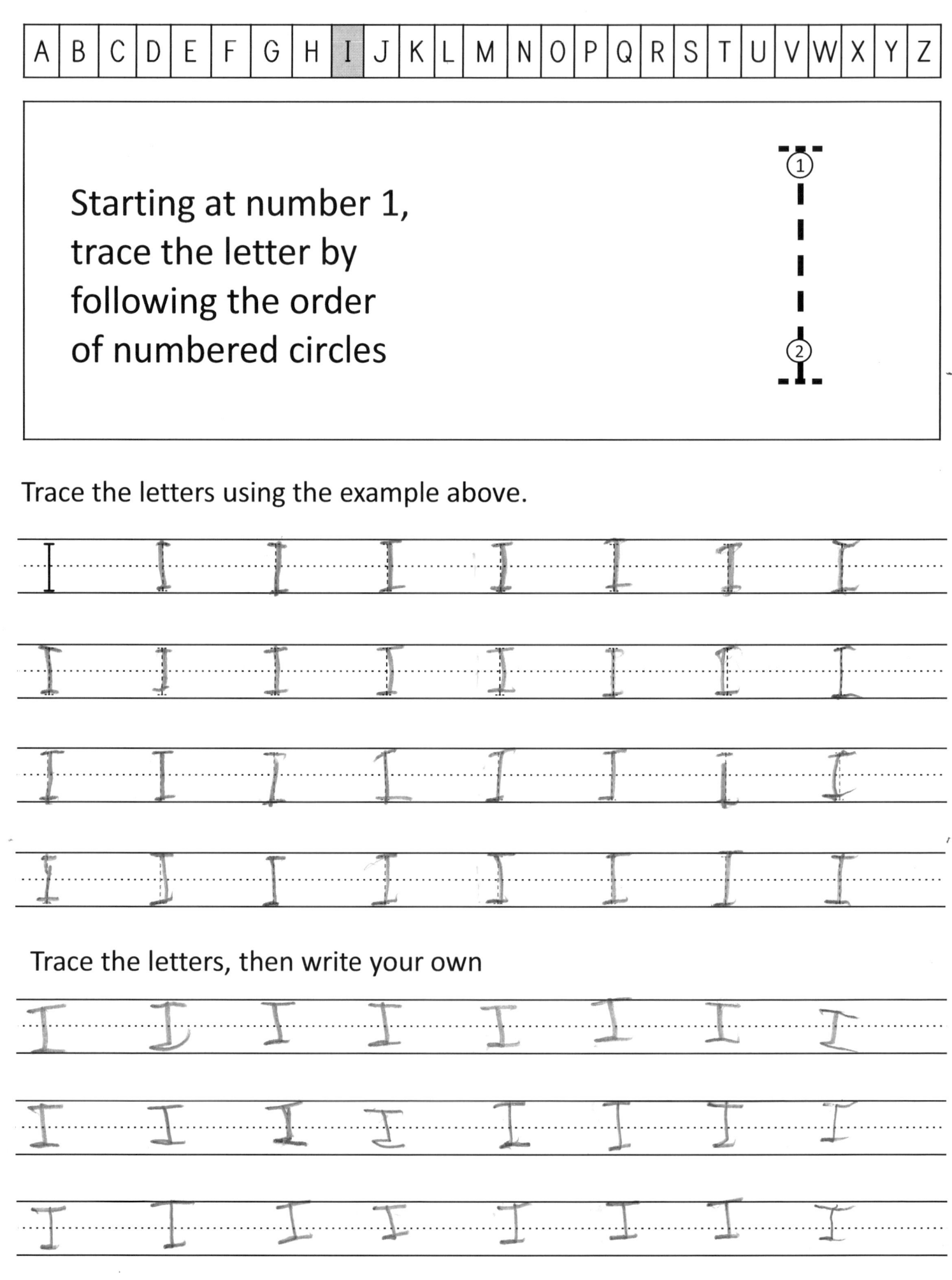

| a | b | c | d | e | f | g | h | i | j | k | l | m | n | o | p | q | r | s | t | u | v | w | x | y | z |

Starting at number 1,
trace the letter by
following the order
of numbered circles

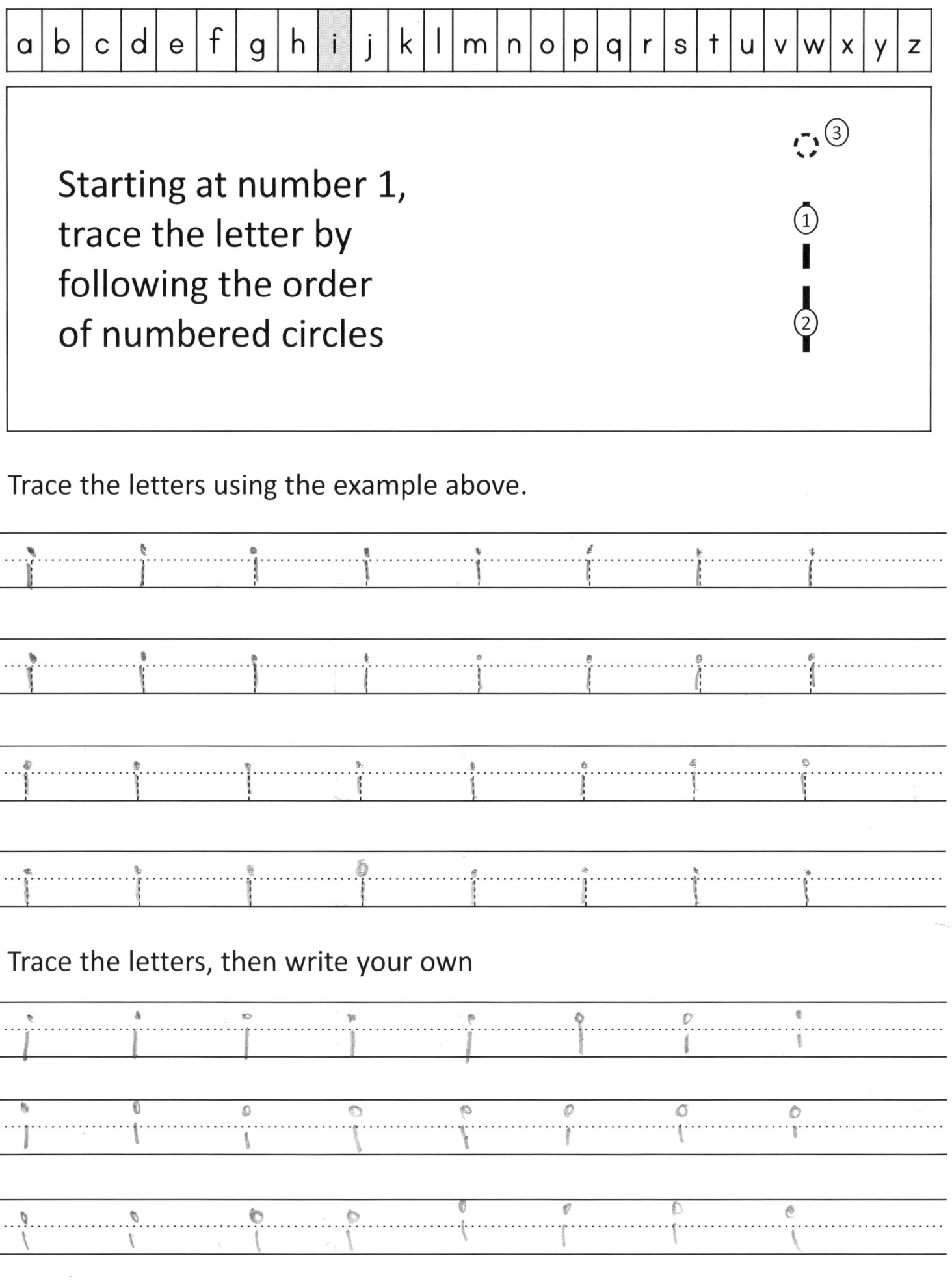

Trace the letters using the example above.

Trace the letters, then write your own

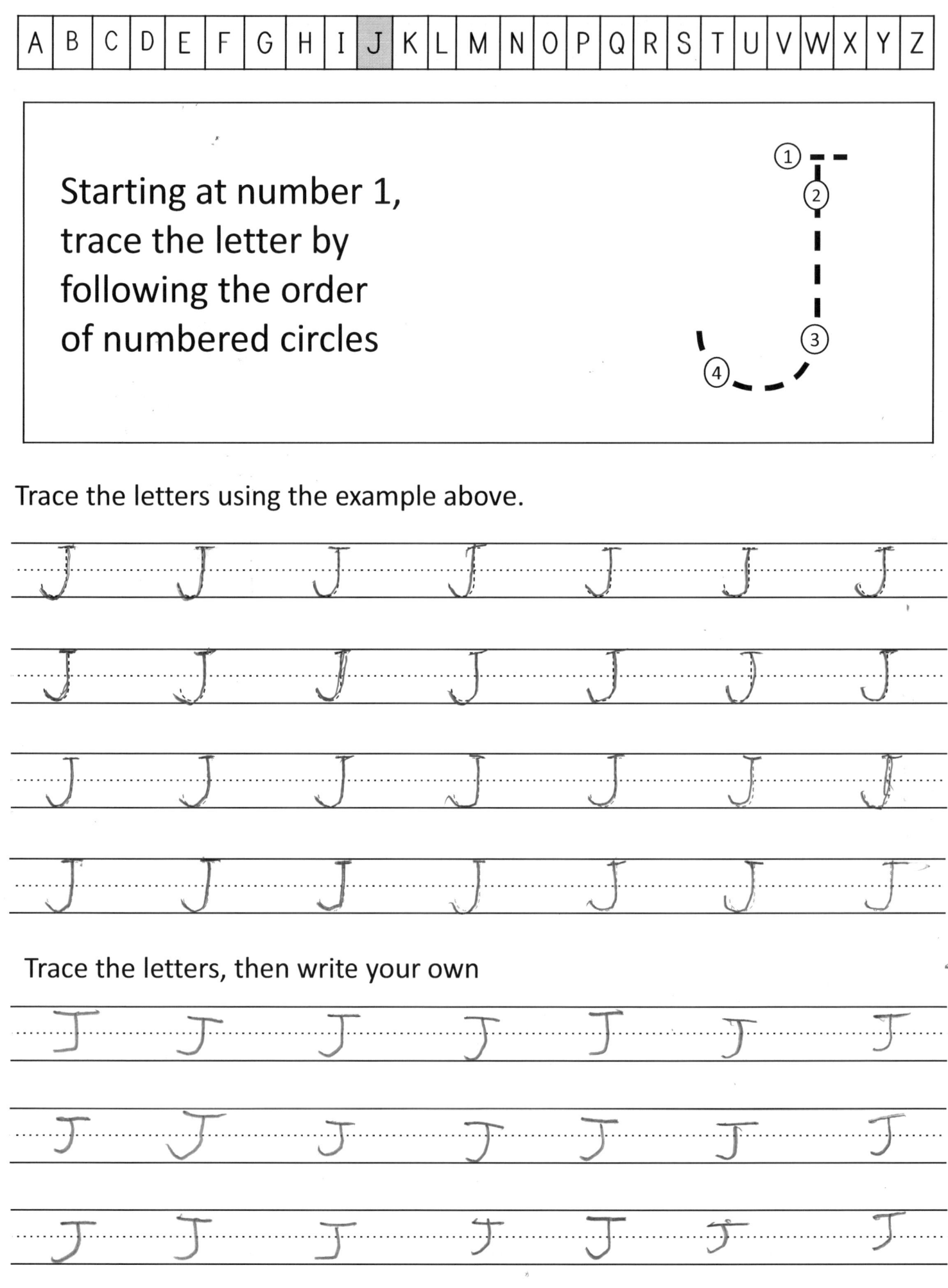

| A | B | C | D | E | F | G | H | I | J | K | L | M | N | O | P | Q | R | S | T | U | V | W | X | Y | Z |

Starting at number 1, trace the letter by following the order of numbered circles

Trace the letters using the example above.

Trace the letters, then write your own

a	b	c	d	e	f	g	h	i	j	k	l	m	n	o	p	q	r	s	t	u	v	w	x	y	z

Starting at number 1, trace the letter by following the order of numbered circles

Trace the letters using the example above.

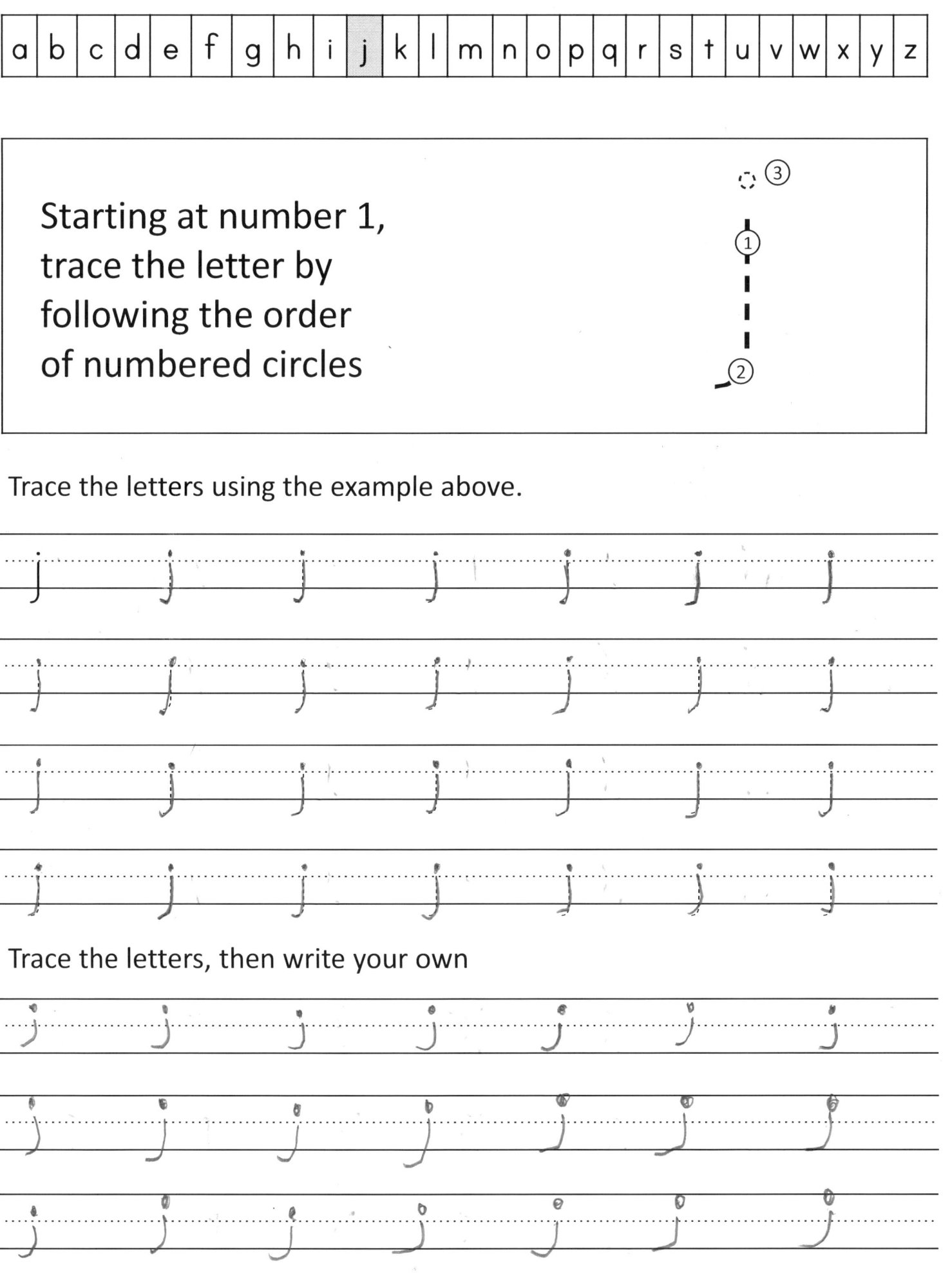

Trace the letters, then write your own

A	B	C	D	E	F	G	H	I	J	K	L	M	N	O	P	Q	R	S	T	U	V	W	X	Y	Z

Starting at number 1, trace the letter by following the order of numbered circles

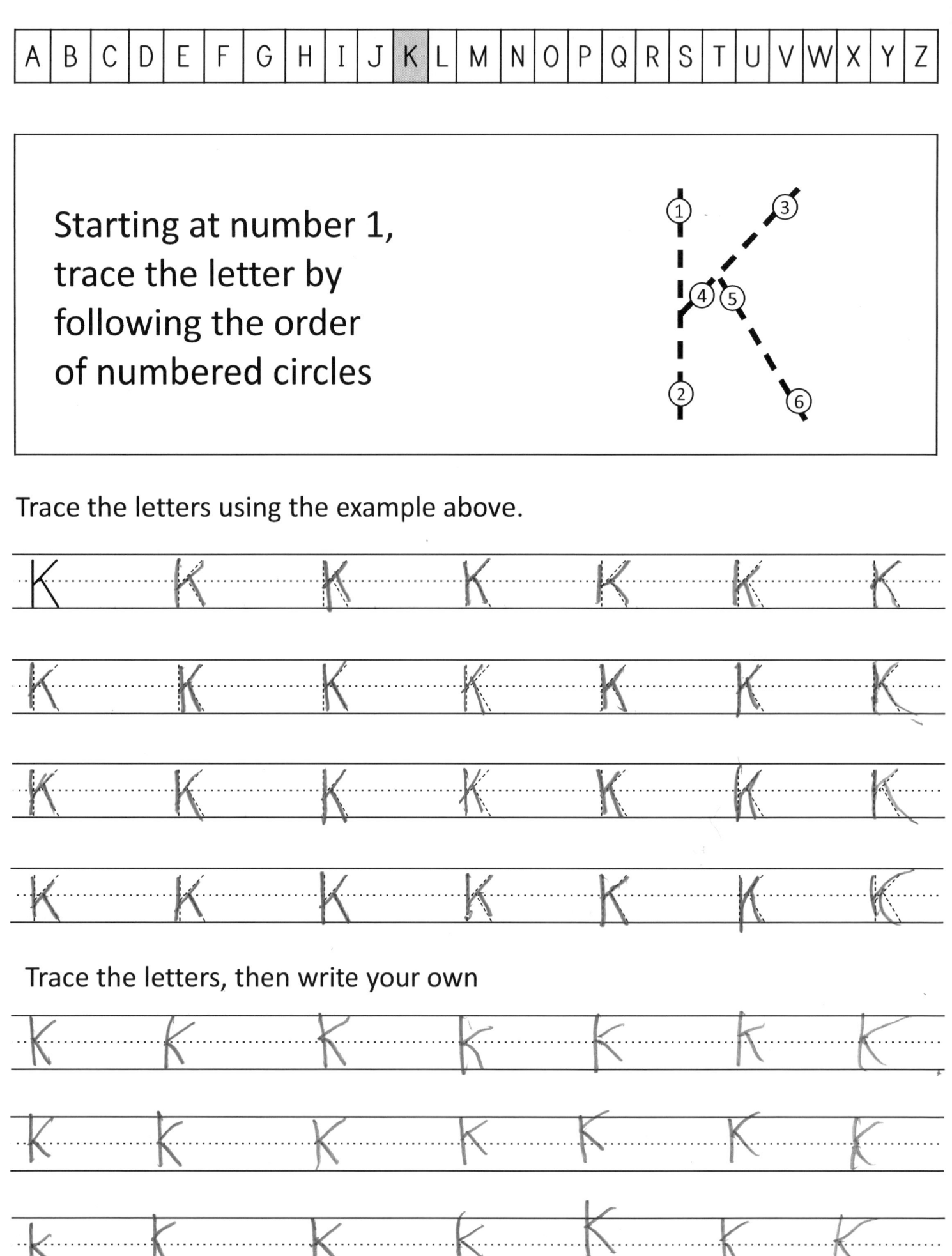

Trace the letters using the example above.

Trace the letters, then write your own

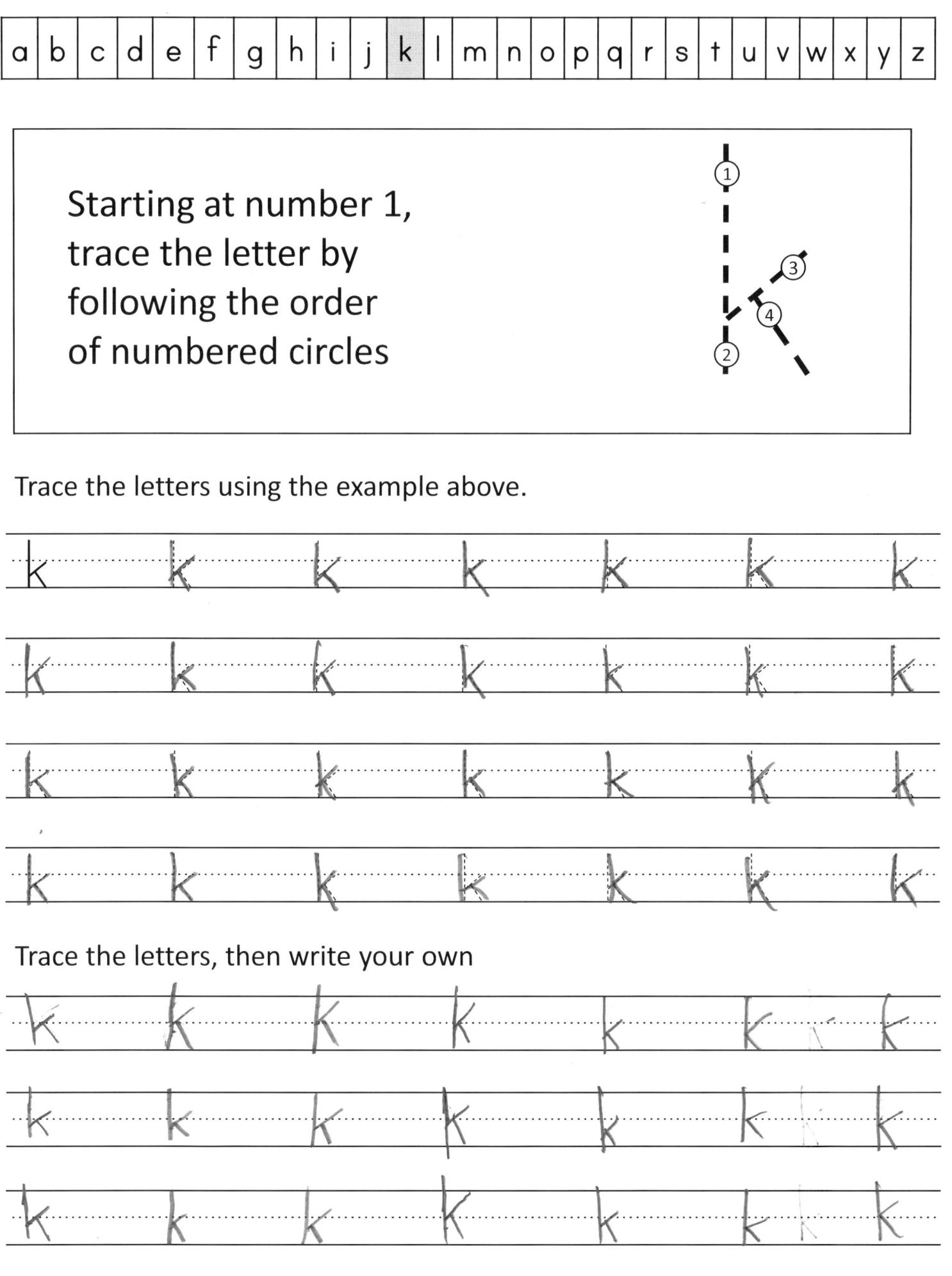

| a | b | c | d | e | f | g | h | i | j | k | l | m | n | o | p | q | r | s | t | u | v | w | x | y | z |

Starting at number 1,
trace the letter by
following the order
of numbered circles

Trace the letters using the example above.

Trace the letters, then write your own

Starting at number 1, trace the letter by following the order of numbered circles

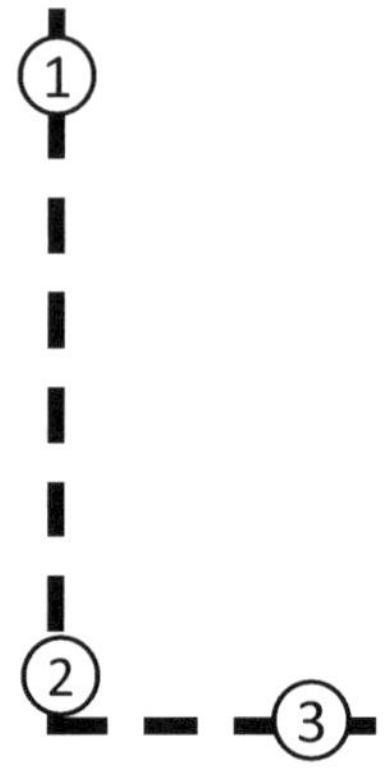

①

②--③

Trace the letters using the example above.

Trace the letters, then write your own

a	b	c	d	e	f	g	h	i	j	k	l	m	n	o	p	q	r	s	t	u	v	w	x	y	z

Starting at number 1,
trace the letter by
following the order
of numbered circles

①
②

Trace the letters using the example above.

Trace the letters, then write your own

A	B	C	D	E	F	G	H	I	J	K	L	**M**	N	O	P	Q	R	S	T	U	V	W	X	Y	Z

Starting at number 1, trace the letter by following the order of numbered circles

Trace the letters using the example above.

M   M   M   M   M   M

M   M   M   M   M   M

M   M   M   M   M   M

M   M   M   M   M   M

Trace the letters, then write your own

Starting at number 1,
trace the letter by
following the order
of numbered circles

Trace the letters using the example above.

m   m   m   m   m   m

m   m   m   m   m   m

m   m   m   m   m   m

m   m   m   m   m   m

Trace the letters, then write your own

Starting at number 1, trace the letter by following the order of numbered circles

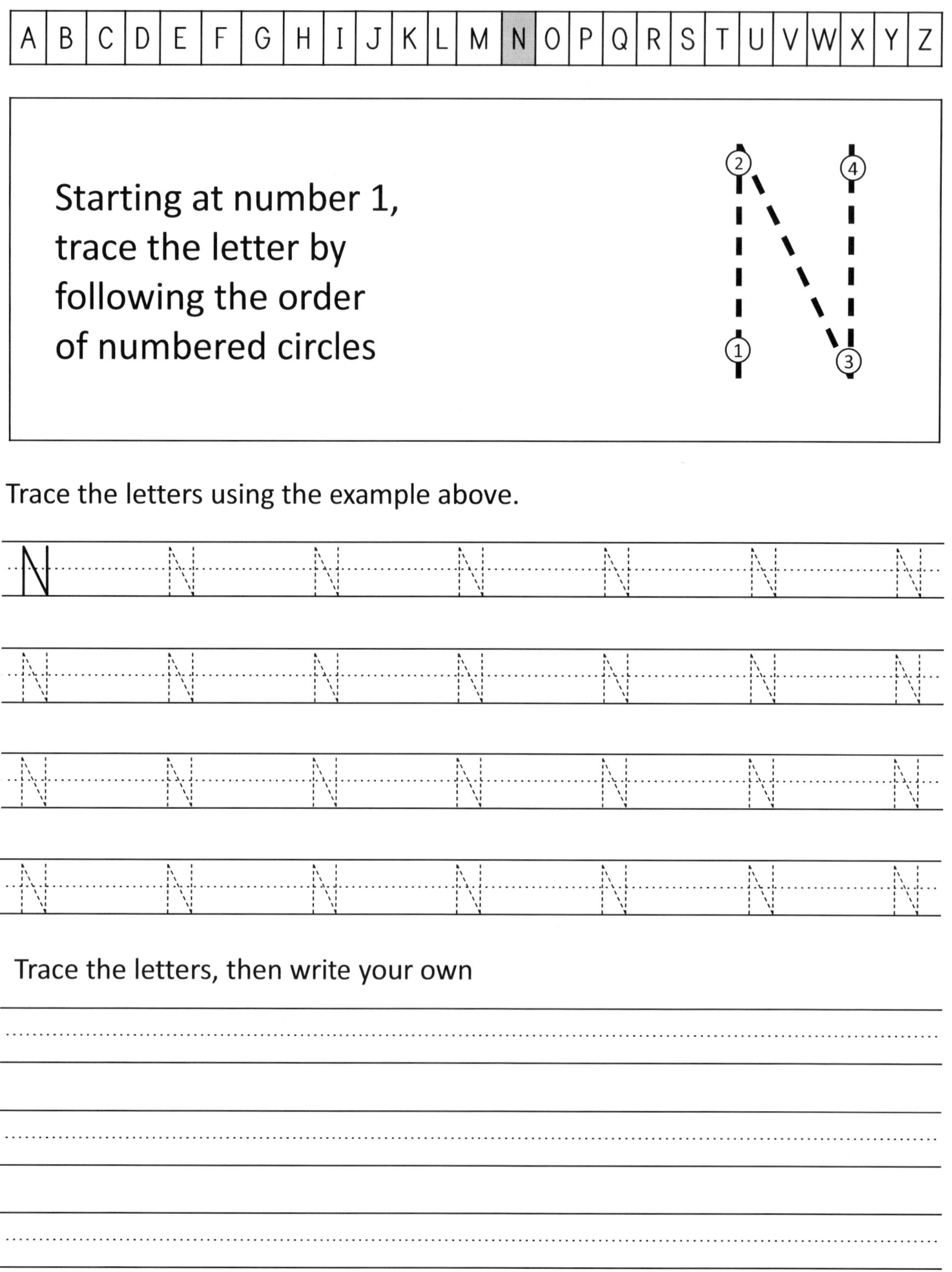

Trace the letters using the example above.

N   N   N   N   N   N   N

N   N   N   N   N   N   N

N   N   N   N   N   N   N

N   N   N   N   N   N   N

Trace the letters, then write your own

| a | b | c | d | e | f | g | h | i | j | k | l | m | n | o | p | q | r | s | t | u | v | w | x | y | z |

Starting at number 1, trace the letter by following the order of numbered circles

Trace the letters using the example above.

n   n   n   n   n   n   n

n   n   n   n   n   n   n

n   n   n   n   n   n   n

n   n   n   n   n   n   n

Trace the letters, then write your own

A	B	C	D	E	F	G	H	I	J	K	L	M	N	O	P	Q	R	S	T	U	V	W	X	Y	Z

Starting at number 1,
trace the letter by
following the order
of numbered circles

Trace the letters using the example above.

Trace the letters, then write your own

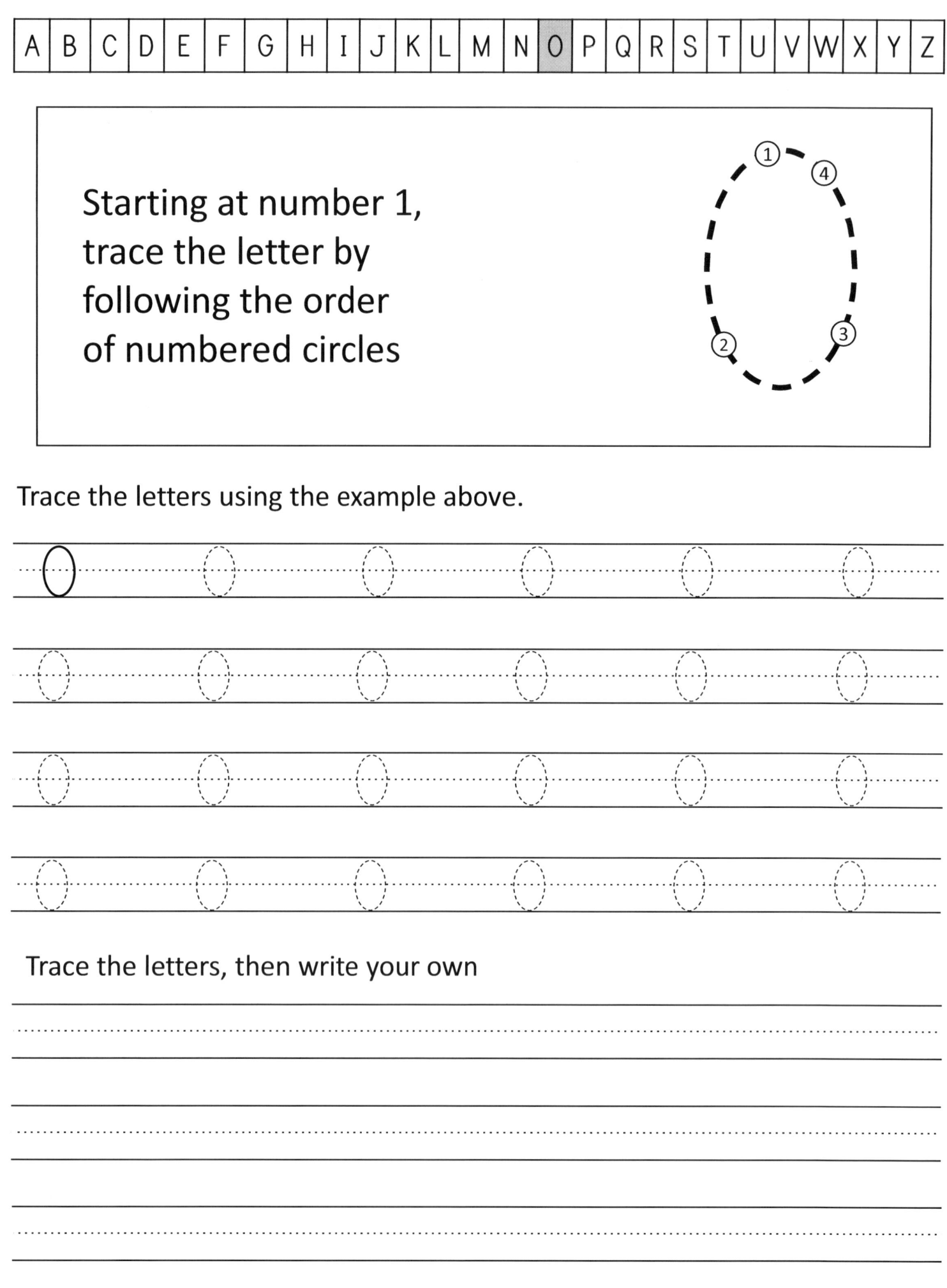

| a | b | c | d | e | f | g | h | i | j | k | l | m | n | o | p | q | r | s | t | u | v | w | x | y | z |

Starting at number 1,
trace the letter by
following the order
of numbered circles

Trace the letters using the example above.

Trace the letters, then write your own

Starting at number 1, trace the letter by following the order of numbered circles

Trace the letters using the example above.

Trace the letters, then write your own

| a | b | c | d | e | f | g | h | i | j | k | l | m | n | o | p | q | r | s | t | u | v | w | x | y | z |

Starting at number 1,
trace the letter by
following the order
of numbered circles

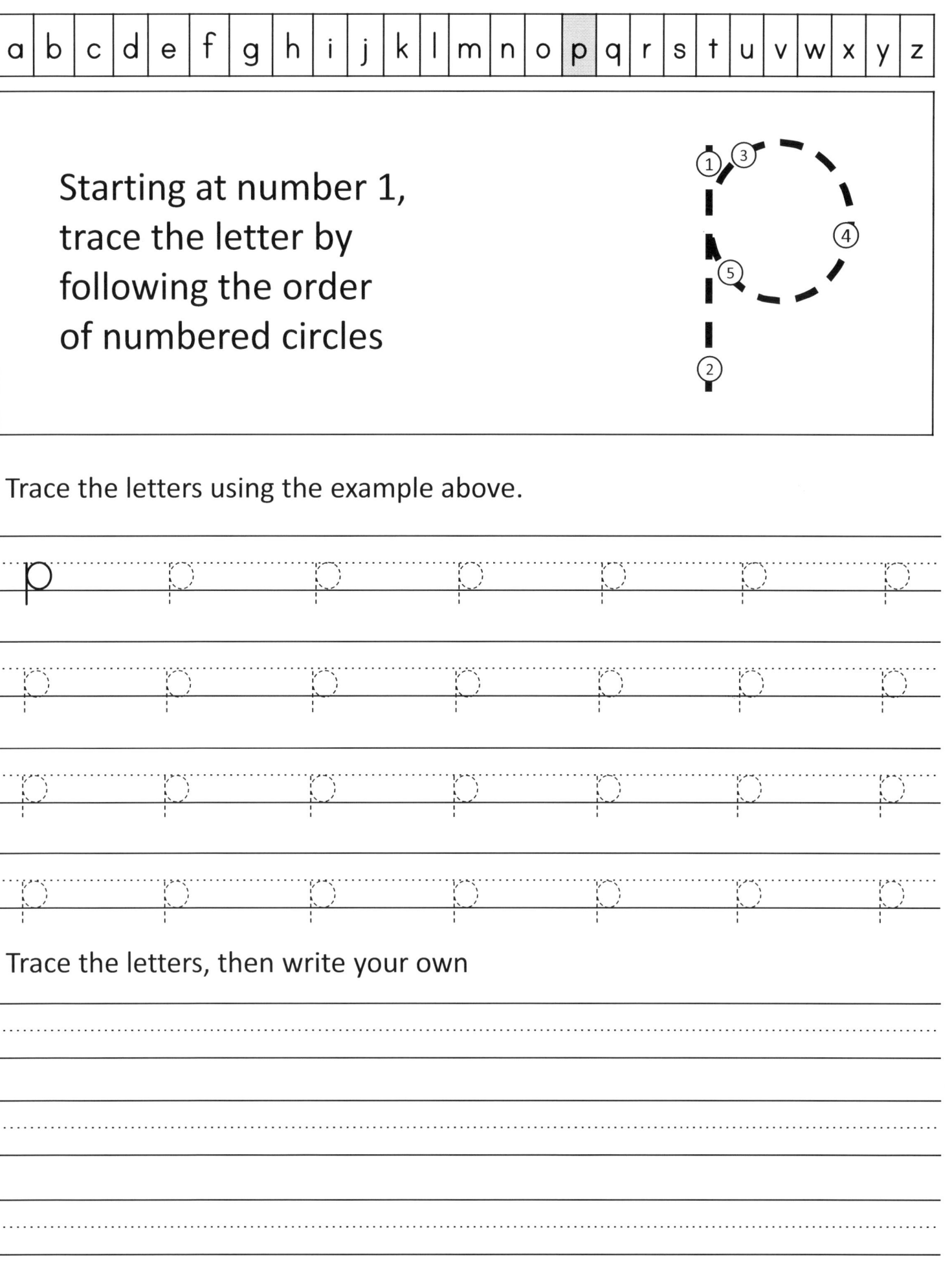

Trace the letters using the example above.

p   p   p   p   p   p   p

p   p   p   p   p   p   p

p   p   p   p   p   p   p

p   p   p   p   p   p   p

Trace the letters, then write your own

Starting at number 1, trace the letter by following the order of numbered circles

Trace the letters using the example above.

Q   Q   Q   Q   Q   Q

Q   Q   Q   Q   Q   Q

Q   Q   Q   Q   Q   Q

Q   Q   Q   Q   Q   Q

Trace the letters, then write your own

a	b	c	d	e	f	g	h	i	j	k	l	m	n	o	p	q	r	s	t	u	v	w	x	y	z

Starting at number 1,
trace the letter by
following the order
of numbered circles

Trace the letters using the example above.

Trace the letters, then write your own

| A | B | C | D | E | F | G | H | I | J | K | L | M | N | O | P | Q | R | S | T | U | V | W | X | Y | Z |

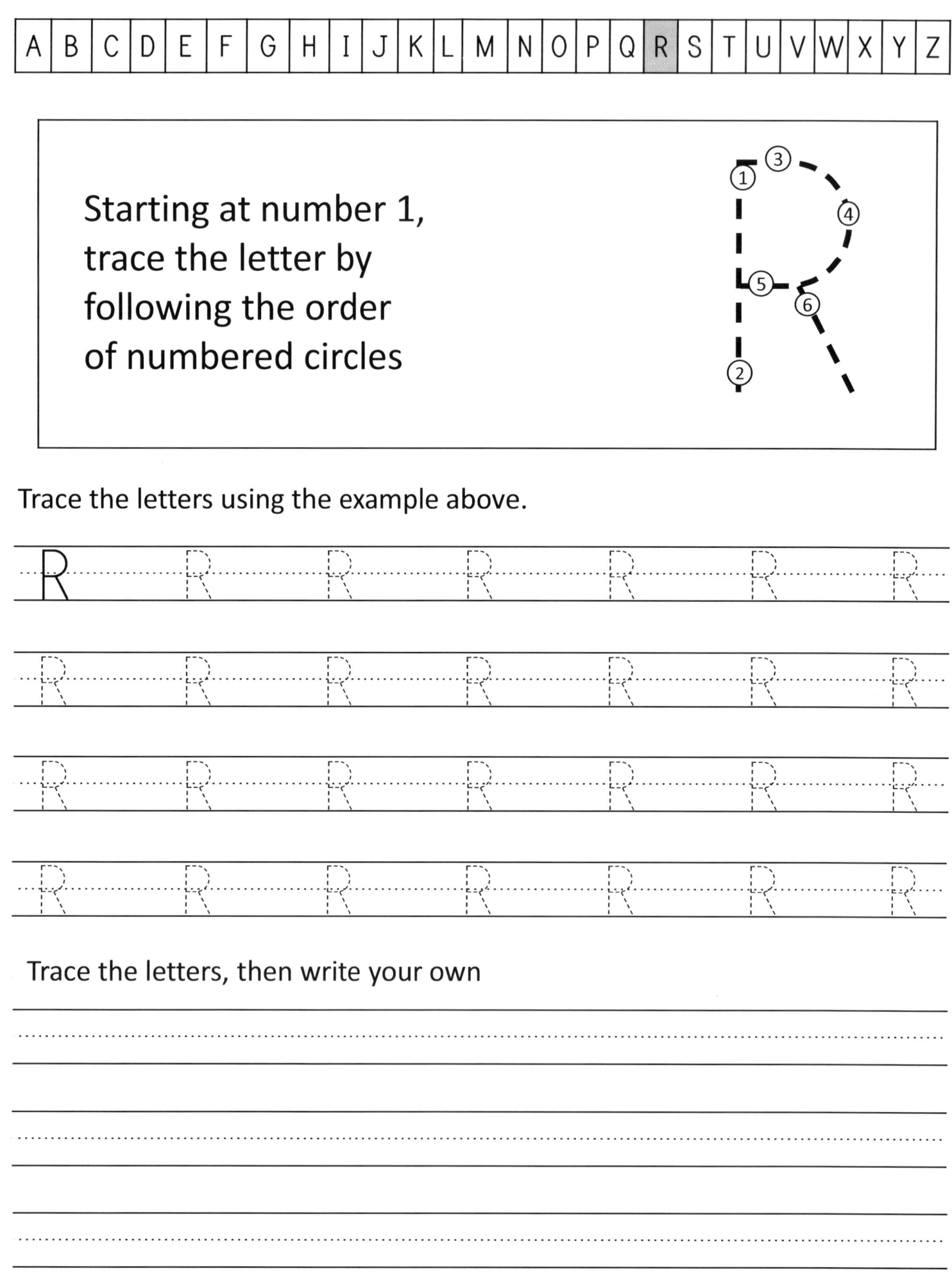

Starting at number 1,
trace the letter by
following the order
of numbered circles

Trace the letters using the example above.

R   R   R   R   R   R   R

R   R   R   R   R   R   R

R   R   R   R   R   R   R

R   R   R   R   R   R   R

Trace the letters, then write your own

a	b	c	d	e	f	g	h	i	j	k	l	m	n	o	p	q	r	s	t	u	v	w	x	y	z

Starting at number 1,
trace the letter by
following the order
of numbered circles

Trace the letters using the example above.

r   r   r   r   r   r   r

r   r   r   r   r   r   r

r   r   r   r   r   r   r

r   r   r   r   r   r   r

Trace the letters, then write your own

Starting at number 1, trace the letter by following the order of numbered circles

Trace the letters using the example above.

Trace the letters, then write your own

| a | b | c | d | e | f | g | h | i | j | k | l | m | n | o | p | q | r | s | t | u | v | w | x | y | z |

Starting at number 1, trace the letter by following the order of numbered circles

Trace the letters using the example above.

S   S   S   S   S   S   S

S   S   S   S   S   S   S

S   S   S   S   S   S   S

S   S   S   S   S   S   S

Trace the letters, then write your own

A	B	C	D	E	F	G	H	I	J	K	L	M	N	O	P	Q	R	S	T	U	V	W	X	Y	Z

Starting at number 1, trace the letter by following the order of numbered circles

Trace the letters using the example above.

Trace the letters, then write your own

a	b	c	d	e	f	g	h	i	j	k	l	m	n	o	p	q	r	s	t	u	v	w	x	y	z

Starting at number 1,
trace the letter by
following the order
of numbered circles

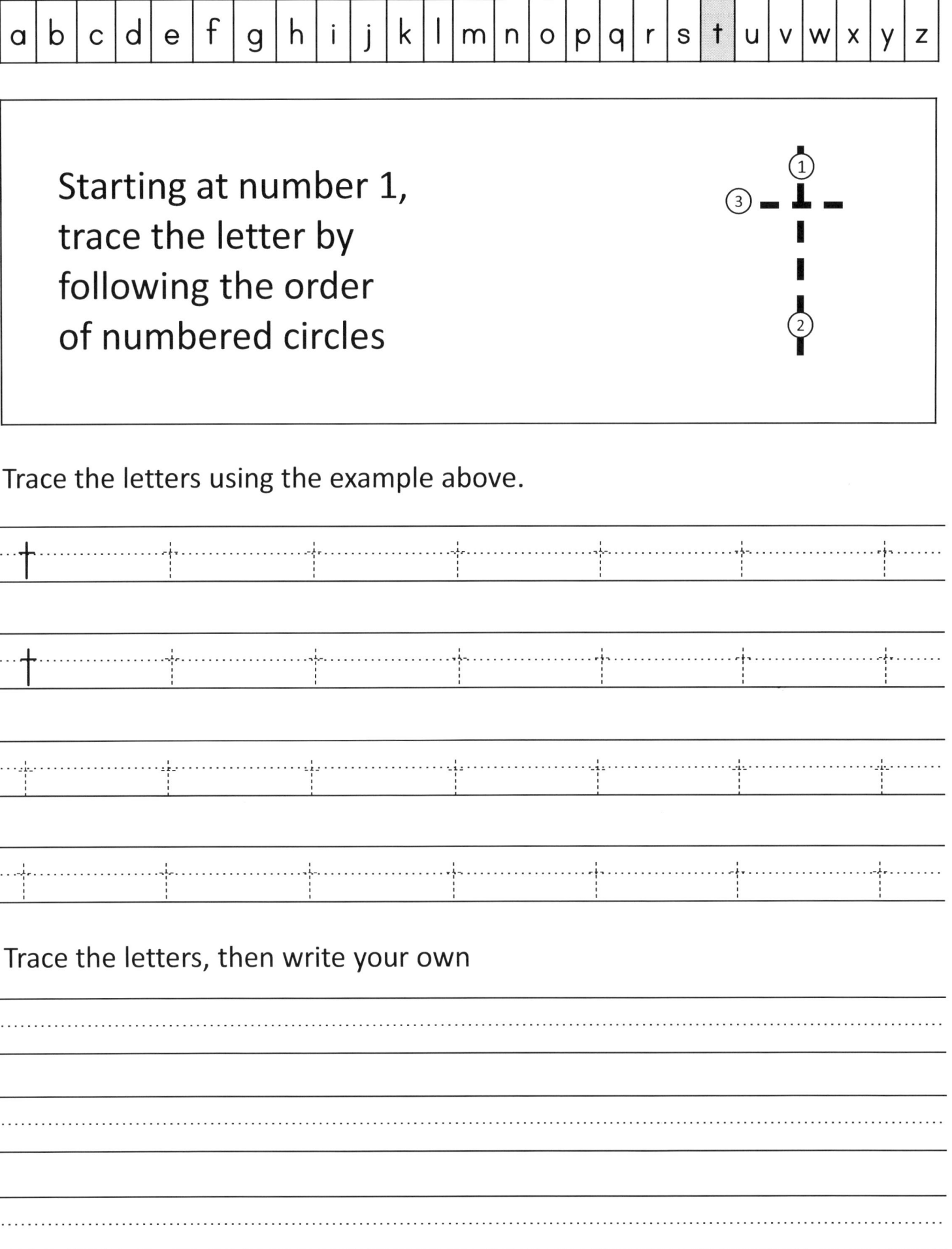

Trace the letters using the example above.

Trace the letters, then write your own

| A | B | C | D | E | F | G | H | I | J | K | L | M | N | O | P | Q | R | S | T | U | V | W | X | Y | Z |

Starting at number 1, trace the letter by following the order of numbered circles

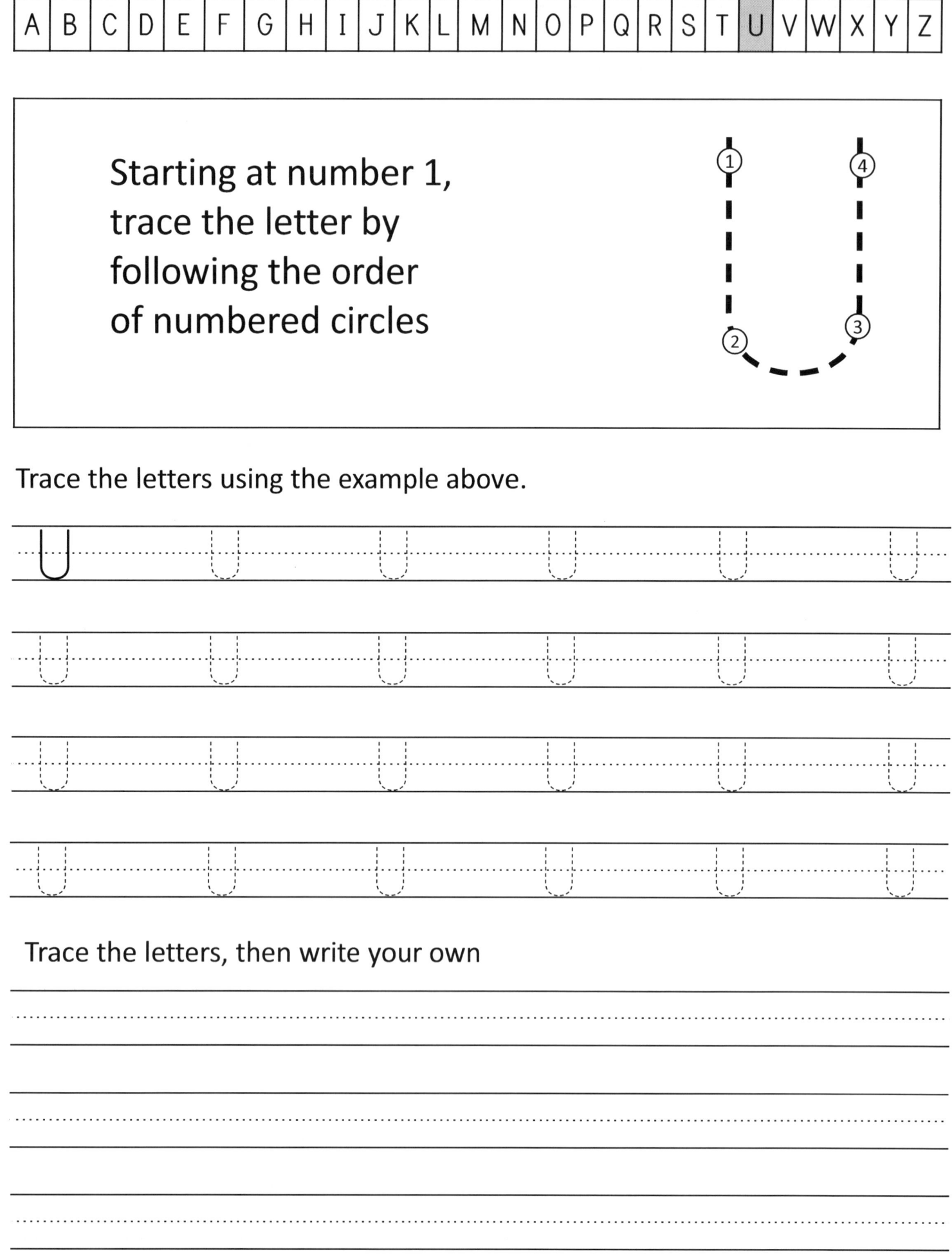

Trace the letters using the example above.

Trace the letters, then write your own

a	b	c	d	e	f	g	h	i	j	k	l	m	n	o	p	q	r	s	t	u	v	w	x	y	z

Starting at number 1, trace the letter by following the order of numbered circles

Trace the letters using the example above.

Trace the letters, then write your own

Starting at number 1, trace the letter by following the order of numbered circles

Trace the letters using the example above.

Trace the letters, then write your own

| a | b | c | d | e | f | g | h | i | j | k | l | m | n | o | p | q | r | s | t | u | v | w | x | y | z |

Starting at number 1, trace the letter by following the order of numbered circles

① ③
②

Trace the letters using the example above.

V   V   V   V   V   V   V

V   V   V   V   V   V   V

V   V   V   V   V   V   V

V   V   V   V   V   V   V

Trace the letters, then write your own

Starting at number 1, trace the letter by following the order of numbered circles

Trace the letters using the example above.

W W W W W

W W W W W

W W W W W

W W W W W

Trace the letters, then write your own

Starting at number 1, trace the letter by following the order of numbered circles

Trace the letters using the example above.

W

Trace the letters, then write your own

Starting at number 1, trace the letter by following the order of numbered circles

Trace the letters using the example above.

Trace the letters, then write your own

Starting at number 1, trace the letter by following the order of numbered circles

Trace the letters using the example above.

X   X   X   X   X   X   X

X   X   X   X   X   X   X

X   X   X   X   X   X   X

X   X   X   X   X   X   X

Trace the letters, then write your own

A	B	C	D	E	F	G	H	I	J	K	L	M	N	O	P	Q	R	S	T	U	V	W	X	Y	Z

Starting at number 1,
trace the letter by
following the order
of numbered circles

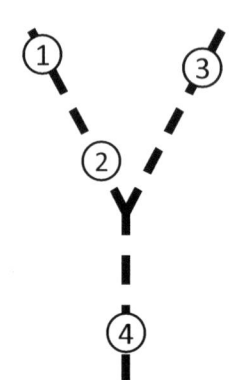

Trace the letters using the example above.

Trace the letters, then write your own

a	b	c	d	e	f	g	h	i	j	k	l	m	n	o	p	q	r	s	t	u	v	w	x	y	z

Starting at number 1,
trace the letter by
following the order
of numbered circles

Trace the letters using the example above.

Trace the letters, then write your own

Starting at number 1, trace the letter by following the order of numbered circles

Trace the letters using the example above.

Z Z Z Z Z Z

Z Z Z Z Z Z

Z Z Z Z Z Z

Z Z Z Z Z Z

Trace the letters, then write your own

a	b	c	d	e	f	g	h	i	j	k	l	m	n	o	p	q	r	s	t	u	v	w	x	y	z

Starting at number 1,
trace the letter by
following the order
of numbered circles

Trace the letters using the example above.

z   z   z   z   z   z   z

z   z   z   z   z   z   z

z   z   z   z   z   z   z

z   z   z   z   z   z   z

Trace the letters, then write your own

Part 2:
writing three letter words

Are you ready ?
Let's go

all all all all all

bag bag bag bag

cut cut cut cut cut

dry dry dry dry dry

end end end end

Write your own words here:

fly   fly   fly   fly   fly

got   got   got   got   got

hit   hit   hit   hit   hit

ice   ice   ice   ice   ice

joy   joy   joy   joy   joy

Write your own words here:

kid　kid　kid　kid　kid

tow　tow　tow　tow

met　met　met　met

new　new　new　new

our　our　our　our　our

Write your own words here:

pen　　　pen　　　pen　　　pen

red　　　red　　　red　　　red

sky　　　sky　　　sky　　　sky

tho　　　tho　　　tho　　　tho

use　　　use　　　use　　　use

Write your own words here:

vet   vet   vet   vet

why   why   why   why

xd   xd   xd   xd   xd

yes   yes   yes   yes

zap   zap   zap   zap

Write your own words here:

Part 3:

writing four letter words:

Trace the words and practice writing
them in the remaining space

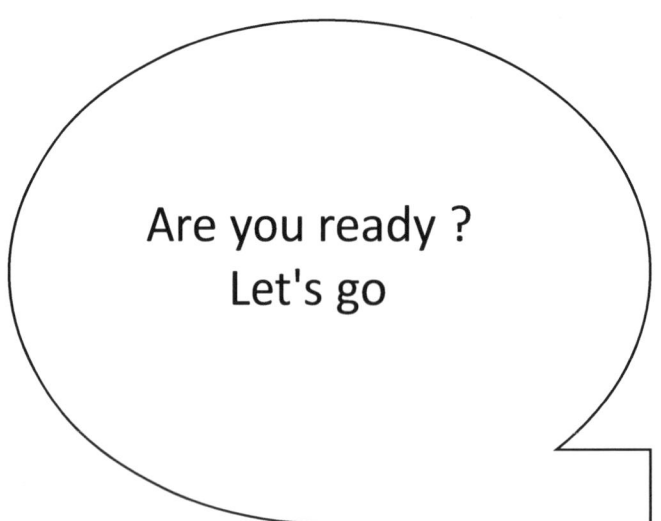

Are you ready ?
Let's go

aged   aged   aged   aged

back   back   back   back

cats   cats   cats   cats

draw   draw   draw   draw

edit   edit   edit   edit

Write your own words here:

fish   fish   fish   fish

gave   gave   gave   gave

hold   hold   hold   hold

idea   idea   idea   idea

just   just   just   just

Write your own words here:

keel   keel   keel   keel

last   last   last   last

more   more   more   more

nigh   nigh   nigh   nigh

only   only   only   only

Write your own words here:

peen   peen   peen   peen

quip   quip   quip   quip

rank   rank   rank   rank

size   size   size   size

told   told   told   told

Write your own words here:

urge urge urge urge

view view view view

wild wild wild wild

xmas xmas xmas xmas

your your your your

Write your own words here:

zeal   zeal   zeal   zeal   zeal

Part 4:

writing five letter words:

Trace and write the words

Trace the words and practice writing
them in the remaining space

Are you ready ?
Let's go

ablet   ablet   ablet   ablet

----

buyer   buyer   buyer   buyer

----

color   color   color   color

----

depot   depot   depot   depot

----

earth   earth   earth   earth

Write your own words here:

fable   fable   fable   fable

green   green   green   green

hello   hello   hello   hello

ideas   ideas   ideas   ideas

jetty   jetty   jetty   jetty

Write your own words here:

known known known known

later later later later

money money money

natty natty natty natty

often often often often

Write your own words here:

paper   paper   paper   paper

quill   quill   quill   quill

reset   reset   reset   reset

sleep   sleep   sleep   sleep

tolls   tolls   tolls   tolls

Write your own words here:

usual usual usual usual

valid valid valid valid

women women women

yeard yeard yeard yeard

zebra zebra zebra zebra

Write your own words here:

Part 5:

writing words starting with a Capital letter

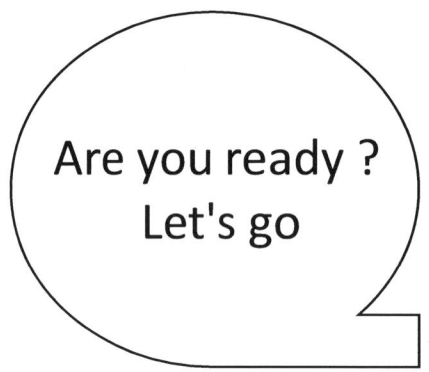

Are you ready ?
Let's go

Are Are Are Are

Able Able Able

Bus Bus Bus Bus

Ball Ball Ball

Cat Cat Cat Cat

Clock Clock Clock

Did Did Did Did

Dull Dull Dull

Ear Ear Ear Ear

Easy Easy Easy

Write your own words here:

Few Few Few Few

Find Find Find

Go Go Go Go

Girl Girl Girl

Hat Hat Hat Hat

Hard Hard Hard

Info Info Info Info

Insert Insert Insert

Joy Joy Joy Joy

Joint Joint Joint

Write your own words here:

Kid Kid Kid Kid

Know Know Know

Log Log Log Log

Lunch Lunch Lunch

Man Man Man Man

Must Must Must

Now Now Now Now

Night Night Night

Or Or Or Or

Option Option

Write your own words here:

Pig Pig Pig Pig

Play Play Play

Quit Quit Quit Quit

Question Question

Rest Rest Rest

Respect Respect

Sun Sun Sun Sun

Seen Seen Seen

Top Top Top Top

Tiger Tiger Tiger

Write your own words here:

Urn Urn Urn Urn

Uncle Uncle Uncle

Vow Vow Vow Vow

Visit Visit Visit Visit

We We We We

Write Write Write

Xd Xd Xd Xd

Xmas Xmas Xmas

Yes Yes Yes Yes

Year Year Year

Write your own words here:

Zeal Zeal Zeal Zeal

Zebra Zebra Zebra

Part 6:
writing Numbers and Numbers Words 1- 20
Learn and practice Numbers 1-20

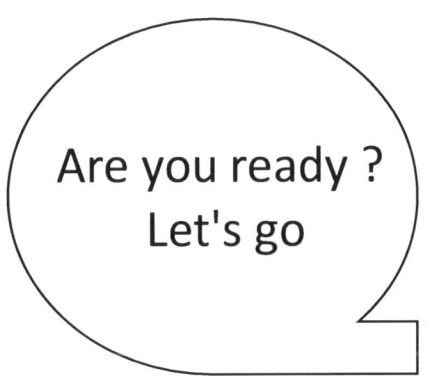

Are you ready ?
Let's go

0 0 0 0 0 0 0

Zero Zero Zero Zero

1 1 1 1 1 1 1

One One One One

2 2 2 2 2 2 2

Two Two Two Two

3 3 3 3 3 3 3

Three Three Three Three

4 4 4 4 4 4 4

Four Four Four Four

Write your own words here:

5   5   5   5   5   5

Five   Five   Five   Five

6   6   6   6   6   6

Six   Six   Six   Six

7   7   7   7   7   7

Seven   Seven   Seven

8   8   8   8   8   8

Eight   Eight   Eight

9   9   9   9   9   9

Nine   Nine   Nine

Write your own words here:

10 10 10 10 10

Ten Ten Ten Ten

11 11 11 11 11

Eleven Eleven Eleven

12 12 12 12 12

Twelve Twelve Twelve

13 13 13 13 13

Thirteen Thirteen Thirteen

14 14 14 14 14

Fourteen Fourteen Fourteen

Write your own words here:

15   15   15   15   15

Fifteen   Fifteen   Fifteen

16   16   16   16   16

Sixteen   Sixteen   Sixteen

17   17   17   17   17

Seventeen   Seventeen

18   18   18   18   18

Eighteen   Eighteen   Eighteen

Write your own words here:

19   19   19   19

Nineteen   Nineteen   Nineteen

20   20   20   20   20

Twenty   Twenty   Twenty

30   30   30   30

Thirty   Thirty   Thirty

40   40   40   40

Forty   Forty   Forty

50   50   50   50

Fifty   Fifty   Fifty

Days of the week:

Monday   Monday   Monday

Tuesday   Tuesday   Tuesday

Wednesday   Wednesday

Thursday   Thursday   Thursday

Friday   Friday   Friday   Friday

Saturday   Saturday   Saturday

Sunday   Sunday   Sunday

months of the year:

January   January   January

February   February   February

March   March   March   March

April   April   April   April

May   May   May   May   May

June   June   June   June   June

July July July July July

August August August

September September

October October October

November November November

December December December

Part 7:

Writing simple sentences and motivational quotes

Today, I will walk through my

fears

Today, I choose happiness

You make me smile

Keep up the good work

You are so helpful

I can get through anything

I don't need to be perfect

I have courage and confidence

I look on my father as a role
model

I live each day to the fullest

I brush my teeth after every meal

My life is getting wonderful
and beautiful

I am sur of myself that I will
fulfill my dreams

I appreciate the effort you
are doing for me

I set goal and I reach them

I love and enjoy everything I do

I give my homework priority

I am worthy of greatness

I am a nice person, I treat

people kindly

You are a wonderful person who

can succeed in your life

Tell me how to imagine success

You don't listen to me

I like to travel with my friends

What is your favourite subject?

If you have succeeded once,

you can train to master better

and better

I appreciate the effort you are

doing for me

"Never retreat. Never explain.
"Get it done and let them howl."
                    Benjamin Jowett

"There is nothing deep down
inside us except what we have
put there ourselves." Richard Rorty

"The will to succeed is important, but what's more important is the will to prepare."   — Bobby Knight

"Action is the foundational key all success"   — Pablo Picasso

"The harder the conflict, the
more glorious the triumph".
Thomas Paine

"There is nothing like a dream
to create the future." Victor Hugo

"Quality is not an act, it is
a habit"   Aristotle

"I like the dreams of the future
better than the history of the
past"   Thomas Jefferson

"The most certain way to
succeed is always to try just one
more time." Thomas A. Edison

"Success consists of going from
failure to failure without loss of
enthusiasm." Winston Churchill

"The greatest source of happiness is the ability to be grateful at all time" — Zig Ziglar

"Do the difficult things while they are easy and do the great things while they are small." — Lao Tzu

"Moral excellence comes about as a result of habit. We become just by doing just acts, temperate by doing temperate acts, brave by doing brave acts."

— Aristotle

"Happiness lies in the joy of achievement and the thrill of creative effort".

Franklin D. Roosevelt

"Appreciation is a wonderful thing. It makes what is excellent in others belong to us as well."

— Voltaire

"Believe in yourself! Have faith in your abilities! Without a humble but reasonable confidence in your own powers you cannot be successful or happy". — Norman Vincent Peale

"If you ask me what I came
into this life to do, I will tell you:
I came to live out loud."
— Emile Zola

Made in the USA
Las Vegas, NV
22 September 2022

55668785R00068